FERRARI 312T

1975 to 1980 (312T, T2, T3, T4, T5 & T6)

COVER IMAGE: **Ferrari 312T.** *(Tony Matthews)*

© Nick Garton 2016

All rights reserved. No part of this publication may be reproduced or stored in a retrieval system or transmitted, in any form or by any means, electronic, mechanical, photocopying, recording or otherwise, without prior permission in writing from Haynes Publishing.

First published in July 2016

A catalogue record for this book is available from the British Library.

ISBN 978 0 85733 811 2

Library of Congress control no. 2015958624

Published by Haynes Publishing,
Sparkford, Yeovil,
Somerset BA22 7JJ, UK.
Tel: 01963 440635
Int. tel: +44 1963 440635
Website: www.haynes.co.uk

Haynes North America Inc.,
861 Lawrence Drive, Newbury Park,
California 91320, USA.

Printed in the USA by Odcombe Press LP,
1299 Bridgestone Parkway, La Vergne,
TN 37086.

FERRARI 312T

1975 to 1980 (312T, T2, T3, T4, T5 & T6)

Owners' Workshop Manual

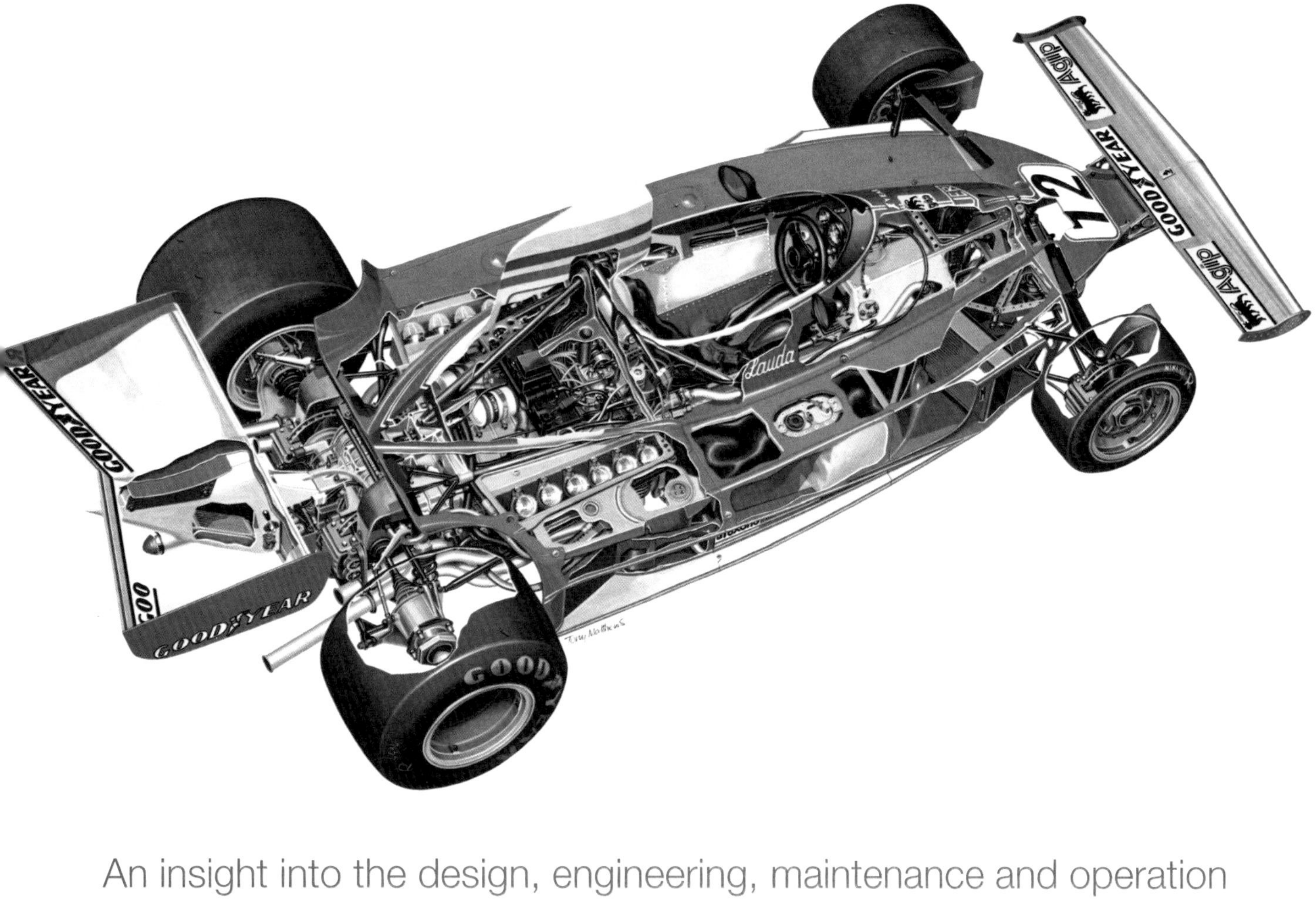

An insight into the design, engineering, maintenance and operation of Ferrari's series of multiple World Championship-winning F1 cars

Nick Garton

elf
4
elf

Contents

OPPOSITE **Clay Regazzoni guides 312T/024 to victory at the inaugural US GP West in 1976.** *(Sutton)*

'Ferrari was an amazing place and Forghieri was a genius' – Niki Lauda, in conversation with Alan Henry. *(Sutton)*

Introduction

The perspective of a young boy from a provincial English town does not bathe the 1970s with much of a rose-tinted glow. It was a time of muddy colours, man-made fibres, picket lines and processed food. But into this porridge-like world came a scarlet flash emblazoned on the front cover of my father's motoring magazines – the weeklies *Autosport* and *Motoring News* and the monthly *Motor Sport*.

Those pictures of the Ferrari 312T series brought with them stories of valour and excitement from the world's great racetracks. To a small boy every racing car is special, but the red cars made superheroes out of Niki Lauda, Clay Regazzoni, Carlos Reutemann, Jody Scheckter and, with the advent of BBC TV coverage, Gilles Villeneuve.

This manual is a guide to the history, design, construction, maintenance and enjoyment of one of the most illustrious lines of racing cars ever built.

It existed in an era dominated by ingenious designs and occasional forays into the surreal – turbocharging, six-wheelers, sliding skirts and fan cars chief among them. Yet for all that, Mauro Forghieri's masterpiece managed to conjure a last hurrah for the classic era of Grand Prix design and construction.

Such a unique provenance makes the Ferrari 312T series one of the most prized and exotic breeds of racing car in the world – and deservedly so.

Acknowledgements

Thank you to Steve Rendle at Haynes for another chance to write about red cars and to Ian Heath in the editor's chair. Most sincere thanks to Crunch Communications for allowing me the time to work on this book; to Peter Secchi and David Wylie for continuing to feed my children, to Sonal Patel for chivvying me along to the finish and to Eric Silbermann for his efforts to try and get something out of Niki Lauda.

For borrowing our star car, Ferrari 312T/024, and his generous time as an interviewee, thank you to Rob Hall and everyone at Hall & Hall for putting the technical meat on the bones.

For their time and patience as interviewees, thanks to Richard Austin, Pietro Corradini, Mark Osborne and Colin Bach. For their time and guidance in whatever form, thanks to Martin Whitaker, Robert Dean, Sergio Rinland, Luca Chinni, Jonathan Giacobazzi, Katja Heim, Rick Gorne, Jacques Villeneuve, Mike Hallowes, Jody Scheckter and the Laverstoke Park Farm team, Ronald Stern, Clive Beecham, Sanja Jovanovic, Ruth Fletcher, Tania Baker, Nigel Roebuck, Peter Windsor, Doug Nye, Phil Reilly, Mike Magda and Mike Sheehan.

As ever, thanks to LAT Photographic, Getty Images (especially Rainer Schlegelmilch) and Sutton Images for capturing our sport with such panache. Thanks to Stephen Lane and Sarah Sorkin at Propstore for the photos of the *Rush* 312T replica, and to Mattijs Diepraam for his brilliant lensmanship.

There are two men who made this book possible: Mauro Forghieri and Daniele Audetto. Not only were these titans of the Scuderia's history the most gracious interviewees, but also generous and meticulous fact-checkers. Alongside them, my humblest thanks to my wife Loulou, all five children and our parents for their infinite patience while I missed a lot of family gatherings.

The quoted comments in this book come mostly from the author's own extensive interviews with the leading participants in the Ferrari 312T story named above. Where they do not, they derive instead from the following sources, which the author acknowledges with gratitude: G. Donaldson, *Gilles Villeneuve: The Life of the Legendary Racing Driver* (McClelland & Stewart, 1989) and *James Hunt: The Biography* (CollinsWillow, 1994); Niki Lauda, *To Hell and Back: An Autobiography* (Stanley Paul & Co, 1986); D. Nye, *Autosport* Nostalgia Forum, April 2002; R. Poulter, *Autocourse 1980–81* (Hazleton Publishing, 1981); R. Smith, *Alpine and Renault: The Development of the Revolutionary Turbo F1 Car, 1968 to 1979* (Veloce Publishing, 2008); R. Williams, *Enzo Ferrari* (Yellow Jersey, 2001); *Motor Sport* magazine, November 1996, May 1997, August 1999, November 2002, February 2013 and September 2013; *The Independent*, 13 July 2009 and 8 September 2013; *The Guardian*, 18 September 2013; *Empire Online*, September 2013; *Legends of F1* broadcast on 'Sky Sports F1', 25 March 2012; ITV *World of Sport* coverage, 1976; the BBC's *Top Gear* website, 25 September 2013; various Scuderia Ferrari press releases; and media materials that accompanied the release of the film *Rush*.

Nick Garton
March 2016

Chapter One

The Ferrari 312T series story

With the passage of more than 40 years it is almost inconceivable that Scuderia Ferrari, today one of the most valuable brand names in the world, was teetering on the brink of oblivion. Yet in 1973 the entire business was in crisis.

OPPOSITE **Until the arrival of the 312T, Enzo Ferrari's legacy hung in the balance after a decade in the doldrums.** *(Sutton)*

ABOVE Colombo's 312B3 in its original, unloved form – here with Ickx at the Swedish GP. *(Sutton)*

A decade earlier, in 1963, Enzo Ferrari had begun to feel the weight of years and entertained the idea of selling his business to Ford. By withdrawing from negotiations at the last minute, however, he had infuriated the mandarins of Detroit, who in turn had unleashed both the GT40 Le Mans programme and later the Cosworth DFV Formula 1 engine to smash Ferrari's hold on the greatest prizes in motor racing. After Ford had successfully steamrollered the sport, Ferrari finally sold his road car business to Fiat in 1969 in order to retain full control of Scuderia Ferrari.

By early 1973, as he reached 75 years of age, Enzo Ferrari's health was beginning to fade and the Scuderia was still no closer to winning a World Championship. In order to protect its investment in the Ferrari name, Fiat began to intervene. The result of Fiat's eagerness for change saw Ferrari's technical guru, Mauro Forghieri, moved sideways to manage the new Fiorano test track, and into his old job came Alessandro Colombo, a designer drafted in from Innocenti.

Colombo decided that to compete against the all-conquering British teams such as Tyrrell, McLaren and Lotus, the Scuderia should adopt British methods. Thus the 1973 car was laid out by designers Giacomo Caliri and Franco Rocchi as a fully stressed monocoque that was then built by John 'Piggy' Thompson of TC Prototypes in Northamptonshire. The chassis was well built but its design was fundamentally compromised, resulting in Scuderia Ferrari's least competitive season of all time.

Following the British Grand Prix, where team leader Jacky Ickx qualified 19th and finished eighth only by virtue of a colossal multi-car accident, Enzo Ferrari gave orders to withdraw his team from the World Championship until a solution to Fiat's meddling could be found. Firstly, he handed day-to-day control of Scuderia Ferrari to a bright young star from the Fiat-owning Agnelli organisation in the form of Luca Cordero di Montezemolo, who became Sporting Director at just 26 years of age. Ferrari's next move was to restore Mauro Forghieri to the leadership of the Scuderia's technical team.

Forghieri conducted an intensive 20-day programme to correct the 312B3's most glaring faults and then the Scuderia returned to racing. After this first small step, all attention was focused on making a dramatic leap forward in 1974 – to which end the popular Swiss driver, Clay Regazzoni, was called upon to leave his current berth with BRM and return to the team for which he had won races in 1970–71. Regazzoni agreed and also encouraged Ferrari to take a close look at his team-mate at BRM, a young Austrian called Niki Lauda. It was the beginning of a partnership that would last for three seasons at Maranello.

New wine in old bottles: the 1974 season

An intensive winter of testing at Fiorano saw Mauro Forghieri rebuild the 312B3. The cockpit was positioned further forward, which allowed him to accommodate more of the

47-gallon fuel load in the centre of the car and thus free up the sides of the chassis for cooling. Forghieri lengthened and inclined the radiators, building them into the bodywork rather than the nose, and fitted long slits down the sidepod to expel heat – an innovative feature that is now common currency in the sport.

Away from the track, meanwhile, Luca di Montezemolo drove a coach and horses through the team's management. Enzo Ferrari still called the shots but Montezemolo made him less remote and stripped away the Chinese whispers that had dogged previous hierarchies; the resulting new sense of purpose in the Scuderia saw its founder considerably rejuvenated. Undoubtedly the greatest change of all to the culture of the team was the cancellation of Ferrari's world sports car racing programmes. Traditionally it was victory at Le Mans, Sebring and Daytona that drove the road car sales and allowed the Scuderia to compete in Grands Prix. Now Ferrari decided to put all of its eggs in one basket, and if nothing else this ensured that the Scuderia went into the 1974 Formula 1 season better prepared and with greater focus than at any time in its history.

ABOVE Forghieri's reworked 312B3 showed the first glimmer of hope – Ickx presses on at Monza. *(LAT)*

LEFT In plan form the 1974 312B3 was a much more harmonious design. *(Schlegelmilch/Getty)*

ABOVE Blast off in Spain: Lauda heads Regazzoni and the rest but was prone to over-exuberance. *(LAT)*

BELOW Forghieri stands beside his 312T, watched over by Enzo Ferrari, as Lauda heads out for the first shakedown at Fiorano. *(LAT)*

At the opening round of the season, the Argentine Grand Prix, Lauda finished second with Regazzoni third. In one stroke they delivered credibility to Montezemolo's management and the team's new-found confidence.

As race followed race, Lauda's prodigious speed was rewarded with nine pole positions and two fastest laps. Unfortunately, his relative inexperience and occasional impetuosity showed through on occasion, resulting in mistakes and accidents that took a heavy toll on his ability to score points on a regular basis. Thus it was the wily Regazzoni – a decade older than Lauda – whose guile and superior racecraft carried him to within three points of the drivers' championship in his defining season.

Mauro Forghieri was meanwhile developing the concept of his 1975 car. His belief that better agility could be wrung from the chassis with better weight distribution had been proven with the 1974 312B3. Now he wanted to reduce the car's polar moment of inertia still further to create the most agile chassis on the grid. To do this would require laying the gearbox sideways across the back of the engine, a transverse rather than a longitudinal unit, that would sit in front of the rear wheels rather than poking out behind the engine with the rear wheels attached to it as was the standard layout. For the gearbox Forghieri turned to his long-time transmission expert Walter Salvarani, who produced the Type 015 *Transversale* unit.

Next came the need for a truly effective chassis. For the new car, the 'English' full monocoque construction was abandoned in favour of a traditional tubular steel spaceframe chassis, albeit one with alloy panels riveted to it

– making what the mechanics termed a 'semi-English' structure. It would be much easier to modify and repair than a fully-stressed skin and would allow Forghieri to build a much narrower, less boxy front end that would reduce frontal area and unwanted drag.

So small was the front of the chassis that the suspension required rethinking completely, with the double wishbones connecting to springs and shock absorbers that had to be mounted centrally and canted over at an angle to fit within the structure.

The first Ferrari 312T was ready in time to be unveiled at Fiorano just before the team flew off to the US Grand Prix. When they returned, all hands were immediately on deck at the test track for another intensive period of winter testing in which the 312T eradicated the inherent understeer that had blighted the B3. It proved to be as supple and responsive as Forghieri had intended – although managing almost 500hp within a relatively small footprint required a cool hand on the limiter. The lap times and driver feedback all indicated that Forghieri had been right to push through with his theory.

The Ferrari 312T and the 1975 season

Scuderia Ferrari launched its 1975 campaign using the 312B3 while sufficient spares to maintain the all-new car were built up at the factory. In Argentina, for the first race of the season, headlines were made by British driver James Hunt and the unique Hesketh with which he led much of the race until he was caught and passed by reigning champion Emerson Fittipaldi's McLaren. Away from this excitement, Lauda finished fifth and carefully banked two points.

The second race in Brazil saw the Ferraris qualify fourth and fifth – and they finished in these positions. It was clear that the Scuderia needed its new car if it was to get on the pace. It would be five weeks until the next race in South Africa, and this would be the debut of the 312T.

In practice, Lauda hit some oil and substantially redesigned his new machine in the ensuing accident, but he still qualified on the second row of the grid. At the start it was

BELOW Lauda, Regazzoni and Reutemann give the world their views of the 1975 Swedish GP. *(Schlegelmilch/Getty)*

ABOVE Passing the baton: the outgoing 312B3 dwarfs the new 312T as Scuderia Ferrari prepares for the South African GP. *(Sutton)*

local hero Jody Scheckter's Tyrrell that got away cleanest and he simply drove off into the distance, becoming the first and only South African to win his home race, while Lauda struggled with a down-on-power engine to scrape home fifth and Regazzoni was forced to retire with a broken throttle.

The Italian press predicted another false dawn for Ferrari. The fault with Lauda's car was tracked to a loose belt on the fuel-metering unit, which effectively robbed 80hp from the engine. With the problem fixed Ferrari invited the media to Fiorano, where it ran Lauda in both B3 and 312T for a back-to-back comparison. After Lauda comprehensively outpaced the B3 with Forghieri's new car the media storm quickly subsided.

RIGHT The local constabulary was much in evidence at the 1975 Spanish GP. *(Sutton)*

Next came the Spanish Grand Prix at Montjuich Park. Lauda claimed his first pole position of the campaign, with Regazzoni lining up alongside him. It was a messy weekend, with drivers threatening to boycott the race due to track safety concerns until the police responded by threatening to impound their cars.

The race went on (after mechanics from every team in the field had gone out to tighten loose bolts in the Armco), but for Ferrari it all went wrong at the start when Vittorio Brambilla's March and Mario Andretti's Parnelli collided, sending the hapless Andretti into Lauda's gearbox. Regazzoni was also caught up in the melee and Ferrari was effectively out of the running. By lap 26, after a number of further incidents, the lead was being held by Rolf Stommelen in his Embassy-Hill when the rear wing failed, pitching him into the barriers on one side of the track before rebounding into the barriers on the opposite side. These barriers gave way, launching the unfortunate German into the spectator enclosure and claiming five lives among the bystanders.

In Monaco, for the next race, Lauda finally hit his stride. He took his second successive pole position, survived an assault by Jean-Pierre Jarier's Shadow early in the race and falling oil pressure in the closing stages to claim victory by less than two seconds from Fittipaldi's McLaren.

The Austrian was in imperious form at Zolder for the Belgian Grand Prix, which saw him take pole position and an untroubled victory. From here the momentum built: he stayed cool on hard compound tyres to work his way through from fifth to first in Sweden and then showed new-found maturity when his old friend James Hunt outpaced him in the Dutch Grand Prix – electing for a safe second place rather than risking all for the sake of three more points.

A flag-to-flag victory from pole at Paul Ricard in the French Grand Prix extended his advantage, but the second half of the season started in troublesome form. A fumbled tyre-stop at Silverstone for the British Grand Prix cost him a points finish. A puncture in the German Grand Prix left him trailing. Then in set conditions at home in Austria he gambled that the early rain would lift and went out with wet tyres but a dry set-up in readiness for a change to slicks. The rain never lifted, leaving him struggling.

Despite these misfortunes, Lauda was poised to take the Drivers' World Championship title at the Italian Grand Prix. His case was eased by the fierce competition between the British teams, with no clear challenger emerging to pursue him. The cancellation of the Canadian Grand Prix due to financial difficulties meant that Lauda had to score just half a point to put the title beyond reach of his nearest rival, Emerson Fittipaldi.

Both Ferraris lined up on the front row and Regazzoni, whose season had been relatively muted, took an untroubled win amid much delirium from the *Tifosi*. Lauda meanwhile allowed Fittipaldi past to take second place, with the four points that he earned for third place being adequate to secure his first World Championship crown.

With the burden of history thus lifted, Lauda won the season finale, the US Grand Prix East at Watkins Glen, with an awesome drive from pole position. After 18 months of hard labour Ferrari was truly back on top of the world, and Luca di Montezemolo was spirited off to sprinkle his organisational magic elsewhere in the Fiat empire, handing over the reins for 1976 to another young administrator, Daniele Audetto.

ABOVE Lauda was in a class of his own in Monaco. *(LAT)*

BELOW To the delight of the *Tifosi*, Regazzoni and Lauda sealed the titles at Monza. *(Schlegelmilch/Getty)*

ABOVE **Lauda leading Hunt clear of the pack – how the first half of 1976 often looked.** *(Sutton)*

The Ferrari 312T2 and the 1976 season

The 1976 season should have been a story of absolute domination for Scuderia Ferrari, who thundered out of the blocks at the start of the year by taking two wins from three starts with the 312T.

In terms of pace, Lauda's nearest rival was his old friend and flat-mate James Hunt, who had left Hesketh to become team leader at McLaren. Hunt had taken pole position at the opening race of the year in Brazil but crashed out due to a stuck throttle. He took pole again in South Africa for the second race of the year but Lauda beat him off the line and headed him to the flag. The circus then moved on to Long Beach in sunny California for the first-ever US Grand Prix West – intended to become North America's answer to Monaco. Pole position, fastest lap and the victory all fell to Clay Regazzoni's Ferrari while Lauda was content to finish second some 42 seconds further back.

BELOW **The 312T remained a potent force at the start of 1976.** *(Sutton)*

So far Ferrari's season was on course, but then Lauda rolled his tractor while mowing the expansive lawns of his new Austrian home. It was a nasty incident that left him with three broken ribs to contend with – and the wrath of the Italian press, who felt that if a Ferrari driver was going to be injured it should at least be at the wheel of a Ferrari.

There was still plenty of optimism at Maranello as it rolled out the first evolution of Forghieri's brilliant design: the 312T2. The most obvious difference between this car and its predecessor was the absence of the towering air intake above its driver's head – these devices having been outlawed after Long Beach – in favour of sleek nostrils in the cockpit fairing. The T2 was a truly beautiful thing to behold when the season restarted at Jarama for the Spanish Grand Prix, but while there was excitement about the new Ferrari there was also amazement at the new six-wheeled Tyrrell, named the Project 34, which featured four small wheels at the front in an effort to reduce the car's frontal area.

Despite the lack of airboxes it was business as usual on the track. Hunt and Lauda were to the fore with the Austrian once again assuming the lead, but on this occasion his British rival held on and fought back past him at the halfway point. Lauda would finish second on the track but in post-race scrutineering Hunt's McLaren was found to exceed the allowed rear wing height and rear track width.

McLaren duly appealed but, until that hearing could be staged, victory would be Lauda's and the British team would be obliged to modify its M23. This redesign temporarily neutered the McLaren threat and two weeks later, at Zolder for the Belgian Grand Prix, Lauda and Regazzoni qualified first and second and finished in the same order.

Monaco was a masterclass in dominance from Lauda. The Swedish Grand Prix saw Ferrari inexplicably off the pace, but Lauda still salvaged four points for finishing third behind the victorious Jody Scheckter as he took what would be the only victory for Tyrrell's six-wheeled car. So far the season was a rout for the scarlet cars: Lauda had scored 55 points and his nearest competitor, Scheckter, was on 23. A combination of poor luck and his Spanish disqualification left James Hunt languishing on just eight points

ABOVE As much friends as rivals, Hunt versus Lauda was an engaging battle. *(Sutton)*

Next came the French Grand Prix, where for once Lauda's luck abandoned him and, after the Ferrari pulled off with a blown engine, Hunt took the win. Soon afterwards Hunt's points from Spain were reinstated, subtracting three from Lauda's tally in the process – and then came the British Grand Prix, where a first-corner crash resulted in a restart and a confused outcome that saw Hunt declared the winner, despite protests from Ferrari (see Chapter Five).

After the debacle at Brands Hatch, Lauda

LEFT Ferrari attempts to get Regazzoni back into the British GP. *(Sutton)*

ABOVE Brands Hatch saw another epic race between Hunt and Lauda while the world went mad. *(Sutton)*

RIGHT *Direttore Sportivo* Audetto and Clay Regazzoni pressed ahead in Lauda's absence. *(Sutton)*

BELOW The centre of attention: Niki Lauda's astonishing comeback at Monza. *(Sutton)*

still led the World Championship on 58 points, but now Hunt – with his Spanish win reinstated – was looming large on 35. Having failed to get Hunt immediately excluded from the British Grand Prix, Daniele Audetto took the Scuderia's protest first to the Royal Automobile Club and then to the FIA – which agreed to hold a hearing in September. By then the World Championship would look very different indeed – and there would be plenty of bad blood flowing on all sides.

The German Grand Prix came next, with the field arriving at the 'Green Hell' of the Nürburgring despite protests from the Grand Prix Drivers' Association that its majestic 14-mile challenge was simply not up to modern safety standards. Niki Lauda proposed boycotting the race but was outvoted by his peers and the teams. Thus Hunt took pole position with Lauda alongside. Then, on lap 2, Lauda's car crashed through the safety fencing, hit an embankment and bounced back on to the track in flames. Lauda was so badly burnt that his survival was at first deemed uncertain (see Chapter Five).

Scuderia Ferrari immediately withdrew from the next race, the Austrian Grand Prix, after unsuccessfully lobbying for the event to be cancelled 'out of respect' for its fallen star – a move that did little to improve Lauda's mood. The Scuderia's red Fiat transporter finally returned to the paddock at Zandvoort for the Dutch Grand Prix with just one car entered, for Regazzoni, who finished second while James Hunt swept to another win, pushing his score to 56 points, just two behind Lauda.

In the meantime, Ferrari had recruited Carlos Reutemann from Brabham. The Argentine star had been required to pay off team owner Bernie Ecclestone in order to facilitate his move to Maranello.

In Italy the race authorities added an extra twist to the proceedings when they judged the fuel in James Hunt's McLaren to be illegal. On race day, Hunt spun out on the 12th lap while trying to regain lost ground. Meanwhile, after qualifying fifth, Lauda dropped down as far as 12th place early in the race, but then began to rally. He would cross the line in fourth, one tenth of a second in front of Jody Scheckter's Tyrrell but more than 38 seconds in front of Reutemann – which made the pain of his labours all the more worthwhile.

As the circus headed to North America, another joker was played: the FIA had taken Ferrari's side and retrospectively disqualified Hunt from the British Grand Prix. McLaren was incensed, with a fired-up Hunt winning both the Canadian and US Grands Prix fuelled in no small part by indignation. And so came the final race of the year: the inaugural Japanese Grand Prix.

The two championship contenders qualified second and third behind Mario Andretti's Lotus. On race day the heavens opened and monsoon conditions set in. In private both Hunt and Lauda tried to get the race postponed. They failed. They raced. Hunt shot off into the lead and Lauda, stuck in the midst of the pack, had a lurid moment on the second lap and that was that. He pulled calmly into the pits and climbed out of the car – unleashing the full fury of Ferrari, the *Tifosi* and the Italian press upon himself.

It was by no means certain that Hunt would go on to claim the title. Indeed, as the track dried later in the race Hunt's tyres began to disintegrate and he was forced to pull in from a hard-won lead and return to the track in a distant fifth place. With two laps remaining he passed both Alan Jones and Clay Regazzoni to take third place, and Lauda's fate was sealed – after all he had been through, the Austrian hero lost the title by one point.

ABOVE Pulling the plug: Lauda tours in gently to retire from the Japanese GP. *(Sutton)*

Politics, personalities and the 1977 season

For 1977 the Ferrari line-up would be Lauda and Reutemann, who would drive a mildly revised version of the Ferrari 312T2. Behind the scenes there were much greater changes. Daniele Audetto returned to Fiat's renewed rally campaign and was replaced as *Direttore Sportivo* by Roberto Nosetto, who was ill-

BELOW Back in harness – Lauda hustles the revised 1977 312T2 in Brazil. *(Sutton)*

RIGHT Having a great day? Probably not if it was Niki, Carlos and Ferrari. *(Sutton)*

prepared for the political hotbed that followed Lauda's retirement at the Japanese Grand Prix.

Of the two drivers it was Reutemann who had by far the better start to the season, taking third place at his home event in Buenos Aires and winning the Brazilian Grand Prix at Interlagos while Lauda continued the lengthy recovery from his injuries.

During the winter, Enzo Ferrari had suggested that perhaps Lauda would have been better advised to sit out the second half of the 1976 season and come back at the start of 1977. That way, he reasoned, the Austrian would have had a good reason for losing the title, rather than pulling out of the last race of the year. In this atmosphere it was suggested that Lauda should step into a managerial role within the team. Even now it's best not to mention that incident…

Ferrari certainly made no secret of putting its weight behind Reutemann, giving him the lion's share of testing duties – much to Lauda's fury. The Austrian pointed to his contractual number one status to no avail and only when he threatened to leave immediately for McLaren did Ferrari relent.

The Austrian then stamped his authority on the team with victory in South Africa – although there were to be no celebrations. At the start of lap 22, the Shadow of Renzo Zorzi stopped

RIGHT Lauda felt that Ferrari had abandoned him, piling pressure on Reutemann in response. *(LAT)*

at the side of the circuit opposite the pit wall, mildly ablaze, prompting two fire marshals to run across the track to douse the flames. The second marshal was a youngster called Fredrik Jansen van Vuuren, keen to help and oblivious to the fact that Zorzi's team-mate, Tom Pryce, was bearing down on him. The Shadow hit van Vuuren at more than 170mph, throwing his broken body high in the air while his fire extinguisher hit Pryce's head, killing him instantly.

From such darkness the circus moved on to the sunshine of California and the seafront at Long Beach for the US Grand Prix West. Some of the pall hanging over the sport was lifted by Mario Andretti becoming the first American to win in F1 on home soil – with Lauda little more than three-quarters of a second behind. Andretti's win came on the debut of Lotus' new car, the 78, which featured ground-effect aerodynamics … of which much more was soon to be heard.

On the bumps of Jarama for the Spanish Grand Prix, Lauda's return to form was interrupted when the pounding he took in the cockpit broke one of his troublesome ribs and he was forced to sit the race out. Andretti's Lotus won again, this time with Reutemann chasing him to the flag.

Over the course of the next ten races, Lauda claimed five second places and two wins, putting the prospect of his second World Championship title within reach. But the results were ground out against a backdrop of internal politics and friction that eventually wore the Austrian down.

As an escape from the toxic atmosphere around him at Ferrari, Lauda had met with Bernie Ecclestone at the Dutch Grand Prix and agreed to race for Brabham in 1978. At Watkins Glen for the US Grand Prix East, Lauda sealed the 1977 title with a fourth-place finish and then flew back to Europe, walked in to Maranello and announced that he would be leaving the team.

Ferrari had already prepared for this eventuality by making overtures to a raw but impressive rookie from Canada called Gilles Villeneuve. The 27-year-old from Quebec had risen through an extraordinary career from racing snowmobiles to Formula Atlantic and Can-Am cars across North America. Villeneuve was a wild, unfettered talent but had impressed

ABOVE Advantage, Lauda. Reutemann outbrakes himself at Long Beach. *(Sutton)*

LEFT Throughout the trials and tribulations, Marlene Lauda watched her man. *(Sutton)*

BELOW Ferrari formation at Monza – although Lauda had a Brabham contract for 1978. *(LAT)*

ABOVE **Gilles Villeneuve brought fresh hope, but endured a torrid start at Ferrari.** *(LAT)*

BELOW **Freed from Lauda's disapproving presence, Reutemann became anchorman at Ferrari.** *(Schlegelmilch/Getty)*

James Hunt when he guested in Formula Atlantic, earning the Canadian a trial race with McLaren at the 1977 British Grand Prix.

Despite Villeneuve's headline-stealing performance throughout the weekend, McLaren boss Teddy Mayer eventually signed the equally promising French driver Patrick Tambay for 1978 – although he retained an option on Villeneuve. Three weeks after Mayer's decision, the call came from Maranello and Villeneuve jumped on the first available flight to Italy.

Although he had turned Villeneuve down, Mayer was not thrilled about the prospect of the Canadian being snapped up by Ferrari. Ultimately the assistance of Marlboro's sponsorship supremo John Hogan was called upon to obtain Mayer's grudging agreement to release Villeneuve – on condition that if he did not immediately sign for Ferrari, then he would remain under option at McLaren for two more years.

The Scuderia intended to enter three cars for the 1978 Canadian Grand Prix, but Lauda was hardly in the mood to go racing. Firstly, he felt no great requirement to continue racing for the team after delivering the championship to them. Secondly, he was furious about Villeneuve being given a third car and diluting the focus at the event. Then it became clear that his mechanic, Ermanno Cuoghi, had been summarily dismissed after it was discovered that he was also planning to join Lauda at Brabham.

Thus Lauda was gone without fanfare or farewell. He simply drove out of the gate and left Villeneuve blinking in the spotlight as he prepared to make his Ferrari debut at his home Grand Prix. The confident newcomer soaked up the pressure but he could not get comfortable in the 312T2.

Before his Silverstone debut Villeneuve had

racked up 1,500km of testing at the circuit in the car that he was soon to race; but Ferrari could offer no such luxury in Canada, meaning that to some onlookers there were times when he appeared out of his depth. The new recruit qualified 17th and crashed out four laps from the end.

Worse was to follow for Villeneuve at the final race of the season in Japan, where he qualified 20th and a frantic attempt to overtake Ronnie Peterson's Tyrrell ended with him cartwheeling into a group of bystanders standing in a prohibited area, killing two people.

At the front of the field, Reutemann's sister car finished second behind James Hunt, but both men leapt straight out of their race cars and headed for the airport, bypassing the podium ceremony entirely. It seemed as though everyone was keen to see the back of 1977.

The Ferrari 312T3 and the 1978 season

Another winter of furious activity took place at Ferrari's Fiorano test track. For one thing Villeneuve needed to get some serious mileage under his belt. For another, Ferrari had switched allegiance with its tyre supply deal, moving from Goodyear to Michelin. While the innovative new radial-ply rubber brought an immediate improvement in the car's handling as far as Villeneuve was concerned, the race was on to break in new components for the latest iteration of Forghieri's 312T series: the T3.

This car was designed to wring the maximum benefit from Michelin's unique tyres. Structurally, the suspension had to be beefier to cope with the increased cornering speeds to be expected from the more effective Michelin rubber and a more aerodynamically effective vehicle.

The T3 looked much more substantial than its predecessors but it was almost exactly the same size as the outgoing T2. The bulkiness was an illusion, but its increased power was not, pumping a healthy 510bhp out of Forghieri's reworked V12.

In addition to its new car and new driver, the Scuderia had another bright young *Direttore Sportivo* in place for the new season – Marco Piccinini, who replaced the much-liked but old-fashioned Roberto Nosetto. Piccinini was a consummate politician and a calm, authoritative presence in the pit garage. His demeanour would come to serve him well.

BELOW Forghieri's 312T3 was the best conventional car of 1978. *(Schlegelmilch/Getty)*

TOP The 312T2 ploughed on into 1978 with Michelin rubber. *(LAT)*

ABOVE An historic moment: Michelin's first win with 312T2/031 and Carlos Reutemann. *(LAT)*

The early season 'flyaway' races saw Ferrari employ its revised 312T2s and hopes were high in Argentina, where Reutemann dragged the car on to the front row at his home circuit in Buenos Aires.

Perhaps he had flattered to deceive with the single balls-out lap, but on race day Ferrari was nowhere and the event was a walkover for pole position man Mario Andretti, at the helm of an improved Lotus 78 with its ground effect now almost fully developed. Reutemann fell away and ended up seventh, 16 seconds in front of Villeneuve at the flag.

Two weeks later, in Brazil, Villeneuve felt more at ease with the car after trying different springs and roll bars to find his ideal set-up. Once again Reutemann hustled the 312T2 on to the front row of the grid and on this occasion he made it stick, launching off the line to pass pole man Ronnie Peterson's Lotus 78 to claim a lead he would never surrender.

So it was that Michelin claimed its first-ever win in the World Championship. Peterson, meanwhile, got a dismal start and fell back, where he soon came to the attention of a charging Villeneuve. For the second time in three races the Canadian's car clattered into the rear of the man he most admired on the grid. Peterson was livid and the Italian and Canadian press were merciless, but Ferrari held firm ... for now.

The 312T3 made its debut at Kyalami for the South African Grand Prix and Reutemann was fairly underwhelmed by his new tool, qualifying ninth behind Villeneuve. The two Ferraris circulated together until Villeneuve's engine sprang an oil leak. He decided to press on regardless, which meant that when his engine blew spectacularly at the end of the main straight, dumping its remaining oil on the entrance to Crowthorne Corner, Reutemann was fairly powerless to avoid spinning off into retirement. The chorus of disapproval gained a few more voices – while Reutemann also had a few choice words for Forghieri about his new car.

The next stop was Long Beach for the US Grand Prix West and the Ferraris dominated qualifying: Reutemann taking pole with Villeneuve alongside him. At the start of the race Villeneuve got away cleanly, but Reutemann was caught by the fast-starting John Watson, who put his Brabham between the Ferraris. The Ulsterman couldn't quite rein his car in for the first corner, forcing Reutemann and Lauda to take the long way round with him and thus handing Villeneuve a clear lead.

For the next 39 laps Villeneuve was unstoppable, but then Reutemann began to make inroads towards him. In his bid to maintain the status quo, Villeneuve made a lunge in the twisty section on Pine Avenue while trying to lap Clay Regazzoni's somewhat intransigent Shadow. The Ferrari was launched up over Regazzoni's rear wheel and into the barriers, handing Reutemann his second victory in four races, while the following day's headlines showed Villeneuve's car in flight with the headline 'Air Canada'.

Reutemann took another pole position in Monaco with Villeneuve in eighth. At Ste Devote on the opening charge Reutemann was once again beaten off the line by Watson and found himself sandwiched by Lauda and James Hunt, requiring a pit stop to fix the resulting damage and putting him out of the running for points. Villeneuve carried Ferrari's hopes until lap 62 when he succumbed to the pressure being put on him by Lauda and clipped the barriers, the resulting puncture tipping him into the wall at the exit of the tunnel.

By now the clamour to oust him was reaching fever pitch – not least because Italy had a new star in the form of Elio de Angelis, a man of genuine potential who had stormed to victory in the Monaco F3 race. In Maranello the Scuderia was now working hard to keep Reutemann in with a chance of the title, and Enzo Ferrari called Villeneuve to one side to ask him, rather pointedly, how much of a contribution he thought he had made to the team's points tally so far. The message was clear: Villeneuve's only duties now were to support Reutemann and get the car home.

At Zolder for the Belgian Grand Prix, Lotus

ABOVE Ferraris to the fore: the 312T3 muscles in at the start of the 1978 US GP West. *(Sutton)*

BELOW Using every inch: Villeneuve attacks in the French GP. *(LAT)*

ABOVE Ground effect made Sweden a private battle between Lotus and Brabham. *(LAT)*

BELOW Reutemann's finest hour: victory at Brands Hatch, 1978. *(LAT)*

revealed its new car: the 79. This was the high point of Peter Wright's experimentation with ground effect and it was in a league of its own. Mario Andretti put the new car on pole and waltzed off with the race. Reutemann started second but missed a gear change, falling back and scattering the field.

From amid the chaos it was Villeneuve who squeezed through into second place and there he stayed until lap 40, when a puncture caused him to pit and rejoin in fourth place behind his recovering team-mate. It was as strong a finish as could have been hoped for while the glorious Lotus 79s swept to an imperious 1-2 finish.

Jarama and the Spanish Grand Prix brought another weekend of domination for Andretti, Peterson and Lotus. Reutemann ran third until he suffered a blown Michelin and was forced to pit. Charging back into contention he went off and crashed heavily, being launched over the barriers but escaping unharmed. Villeneuve also had to pit with ruined tyres and came home in a muted tenth place.

The Swedish Grand Prix brought with it a sensation in the form of Gordon Murray's amazing 'fan car'. The Brabham BT46B featured a large fan at the rear, allegedly for cooling purposes but in fact used to pull air out from under the car, sucking it down on to the track. It was brilliant and it worked – sparking protests from rival teams who declared it to be a moveable aerodynamic device and were also rather miffed about the stones, rubber and other debris that the fan spat out at anyone immediately behind it.

Niki Lauda gave the BT46B its first and only victory in front of Andretti's Lotus. In a race that was all about downforce the Ferraris qualified

ABOVE **Villeneuve reined in the excesses to contribute points while Reutemann pressed on.** *(Schlegelmilch/Getty)*

seventh and eighth and finished ninth and tenth, never troubling the British teams unduly.

The 'fan car' was outlawed by the time of the French Grand Prix at Paul Ricard but Brabham was still strong. Some jousting went on between Andretti, Watson, Lauda and Peterson but the Lotus drivers prevailed for another 1-2 with Lauda's engine blowing and Watson being pushed down to fourth by an inspired James Hunt. The Ferraris were nowhere near the pace and finished 12th (Villeneuve) and 18th (Reutemann).

The British Grand Prix at Brands Hatch saw the Ferraris struggle in qualifying, prompting Michelin to fly out a new compound on Saturday night, requiring the mechanics to work late on set-up changes, including Reutemann's request to use a narrower front track, while Villeneuve retained the wider track and lower-profile front tyres.

The narrow, twisty undulations were not an obvious match to Forghieri's 312T3 and it was expected that the British teams would run away with the race once again. Yet both of the Lotuses broke while leading, as did Jody Scheckter's Wolf and Alan Jones' Williams. Reutemann, meanwhile, discovered that his pace increased as the race went on, catching Niki Lauda's Brabham and forcing his way through to take a lead that he would not surrender. This victory elevated Reutemann back to third in the title race, 14 points away from Mario Andretti.

The championship was, however, decided by a run of three wins for Lotus – two for Andretti and one for Peterson – in Germany, Austria and Holland. Neither of the Ferrari drivers had a car that could challenge the Lotus. Perhaps it was therefore Enzo Ferrari's way of incentivising the drivers when he allowed Jody Scheckter to hold a press conference in Germany, at which he announced that he would be joining Scuderia Ferrari in 1979.

Villeneuve was worried about his future but made the podium in Austria after Reutemann

Motorcraft
GOODYEAR

was excluded for receiving outside assistance when marshals push-started him from a dangerous position. Uncertainty about the following year did little to improve team spirits or results; but then, after the Dutch Grand Prix, Reutemann held his own press conference. He would be replacing Ronnie Peterson at Lotus in 1979 – Villeneuve would remain at Maranello alongside Scheckter.

Then came the Italian Grand Prix, at which Andretti expected to be crowned champion with Peterson dutifully covering his tail. Andretti took pole position but it was Villeneuve who would line up alongside him, with the powerful Renault turbo of Jean-Pierre Jabouille in third and Lauda's Brabham fourth. Peterson's role as wingman would be compromised by starting from fifth and, worse, he crashed his Lotus 79 heavily in the warm-up, requiring a switch to the spare car – an old Lotus 78.

At the start Andretti and Villeneuve sprinted away with Jabouille and Lauda close at hand, but in their wake Jones' Williams, Watson's Brabham, Laffite's Ligier, Scheckter's Wolf, Peterson's Lotus and Hunt's McLaren were squabbling, and into this mix came the new Italian star Riccardo Patrese in his fast-starting Shadow.

Patrese had come thundering down the wrong side of the white line on the run towards the chicane at the entrance to Curva Grande and Hunt did not want to give him space to rejoin the pack. The two cars collided, bouncing Hunt into Peterson, whose Lotus speared left into the barriers, where it was torn in half and burst into flames before rebounding on to the track as chaos erupted throughout the following pack.

Reutemann's Ferrari, the Shadows of Clay Regazzoni and Hans Stuck, the Tyrrells of Didier Pironi and Patrick Depailler, Vittorio Brambilla's Surtees, Derek Daly's Ensign and Brett Lunger's McLaren were all caught up in the melée. Peterson was trapped in his burning car with both his legs badly broken and it took fast work by Hunt, Regazzoni and Depailler to brave the fire and pull him out of the wreckage. At the side of the track, Brambilla was unconscious and Stuck was dazed after they were both hit on the head by stray wheels. The race was immediately stopped.

Finally, at 6pm the race was restarted over a shortened 40-lap distance and from the front row Villeneuve jumped the start, taking Andretti with him. Both men were given one-minute penalties, putting them back to sixth (Andretti) and seventh

OPPOSITE Tragedy plays out in the wake of fast-starting Villeneuve, Monza 1978. *(Sutton)*

LEFT Villeneuve and Andretti lead away the restarted Italian GP. *(Sutton)*

(Villeneuve) in the classified results. That single point for Andretti would be sufficient to clinch the championship because the following morning Peterson, having suffered a blood clot in his injured legs, suffered a fatal aneurysm.

Amid much rancour, the Grand Prix Drivers' Association adjudged that Patrese was at fault and banned him from taking part in the US Grand Prix at Watkins Glen. The race was won sublimely by Carlos Reutemann's Ferrari, with Villeneuve losing a secure second place when his engine dropped a piston.

The season finale came in Montréal on an all-new circuit in the middle of the St Lawrence River for the Canadian Grand Prix. A year on from his Ferrari debut, Villeneuve was finding his feet. He lined up third on the grid behind Lotus replacement driver Jean-Pierre Jarier and the Wolf of Jody Scheckter. On a bitterly cold day Jarier's Lotus did the best job of putting heat into its tyres as the superior ground effect came into play and he stayed in front for 50 laps until his brakes failed and he pulled into the pits.

Villeneuve, having dispatched Scheckter, thus inherited the lead and counted down the laps in front of an enraptured home crowd. Snow was beginning to fall as he crossed the line, and on the podium his diminutive frame was swamped by a vast anorak to keep out the cold. He stood, somewhat overawed by the occasion, between Scheckter and third-placed Carlos Reutemann. It was like the changing of the guard.

The Ferrari 312T4 and the 1979 season

Jody Scheckter was a familiar face in the Ferrari set-up long before he had signed a contract. Enzo Ferrari had tried to sign him during his debut season of 1973 but the canny South African decided that entering the maelstrom of Maranello was not what he needed so early in his career and went instead to Tyrrell, where nurture was in healthy supply.

From Tyrrell, the young South African moved to the start-up operation of Wolf. Team owner Walter Wolf was such a good customer and advocate for Ferrari's road cars that his team had often been welcomed to test at Fiorano. Scheckter was an impressive driver and a strong leader – and midway through 1978 he decided that the timing was now right to take the biggest job in the sport as Number One at Scuderia Ferrari.

Laconic to the point of disinterest, Scheckter had developed a professional approach to racing that closely mirrored Niki Lauda's. All the fanfare

RIGHT At last! Villeneuve stands tall after victory at home, flanked by past and future teammates. *(LAT)*

and jamboree that accompanied successful Formula 1 drivers left him cold and when it came to the innate passion that Ferrari inspired his approach was no different. He would brush off the impassioned cheers, waves and 'Forza Ferraris' of the *Tifosi* with a deadpan 'Yeah, Forza.'

Setting an example that would be echoed a couple of decades later by Michael Schumacher, Scheckter kept himself in trim with a strict exercise regime, drove carefully to the factory, diligently checked and rechecked everything from flight schedules to tyre compounds, held meetings with Forghieri and Piero Ferrari and drove his test sessions with focus and stern-eyed attention.

By contrast Villeneuve would arrive wreathed in tyre smoke and boasting of his latest record time to Maranello from his home on the Côte d'Azur – and then, after joking around with the mechanics, would cheerfully jump in the car and drive it for all it was worth.

ABOVE The 1979 steamroller: Scheckter in front of Villeneuve. *(Schlegelmilch/Getty)*

BELOW Ferrari's two stars gelled despite their different approaches to racing. *(Schlegelmilch/Getty)*

The two drivers had a considerable job on their hands to help Forghieri challenge the all-conquering ground-effect cars being built in Britain. Having begun to fit side skirts to the Ferrari 312T3s late in the 1978 season, Forghieri focused on the dark art of aerodynamics as never before with the design for 1979. Fundamentally, the architecture of the chassis was little changed from the T3 to the T4, but how it interacted with the air moving around it would be radically rethought.

After belatedly gaining permission from Enzo Ferrari to pursue the ground-effect path – the Old Man mocking him for his apparent fixation with 'skirts', telling him that they should be kept on ladies and the shorter the better – Forghieri went to work. He recruited Fiat and Pininfarina, using their wind tunnels and technology to hone the most aerodynamically effective shape possible.

Michelin worked hard on its tyre compounds (although Scheckter never felt that they shared sufficient knowledge with the team), and Forghieri developed a whole new suite of front and rear wings. More grip had to be found from using the upper structures of the car rather than the chassis floor because the broad V12 engine worked against creating the swept venturis upon which the concept hinged. A narrow Cosworth V8 or Renault V6 turbo was infinitely better proportioned for that job – but neither engine could combine the power and reliability of Forghieri's brilliant V12, even in its tenth season.

That brilliant engine was also given a major overhaul, however. It made use of new alloys in its construction that shaved a whopping 26kg from its bulk, yet the Ferrari engine shop also managed to coax its output up to 515bhp.

BELOW The 312T3 did sterling work into 1979. *(Sutton)*

The resulting car, the Ferrari 312T4, looked like a manta ray from some angles and a wheelbarrow from others. For the opening races of the year, however, the old T3 was left to carry the weight of expectation in the 'flyaway' rounds of South America, as was Ferrari's habit. In Argentina it was expected that the Lotus pairing of Mario Andretti and Carlos Reutemann would hold sway – the Lotus 79s having been repainted from the black and gold of JPS to a dark green in deference to Martini sponsorship – but it was not to be.

Other teams had improved upon the Lotus ground-effect concept and it was Ligier that held the front row in qualifying, with Jacques Laffite and Patrick Depailler. Laffite took an easy win while Scheckter crashed out at the start and Villeneuve's engine failed.

A second successive win followed for Laffite in Brazil, where the Ferraris finished fifth and sixth, one lap down. In South Africa the new 312T4s were ready and showed their promise by qualifying second and third. The race started on a wet track, and Villeneuve, on wet tyres, took the early lead before pitting for slicks. Scheckter then led, having started the race on slicks, but he had beaten the life out of them just staying on the track in the early laps and thus also had to call in for new rubber. Scheckter reluctantly handed the lead back to Villeneuve – who duly won.

At Long Beach, Villeneuve took his first-ever pole position. Despite messing up the start procedure, earning himself a fine and forcing everyone to do a second formation lap, he romped off to a dominant victory with Scheckter hanging on grimly in second place. Suddenly the Ferraris looked unstoppable.

Upon F1's return to Europe for the Spanish Grand Prix, however, the Ligiers were back on form and Patrick Depailler won after Laffite's engine blew. Villeneuve should have come second but he crashed out while trying to pass Reutemann's Lotus, leaving Scheckter to uphold Ferrari honours in fourth.

At the Belgian Grand Prix both Ferraris were involved in an early altercation with Clay

Regazzoni's Williams that put the Swiss driver out and forced Villeneuve to pit for a new nosecone and front wing. He charged back through the field, regaining a lap, but then ran out of fuel on the last lap. Scheckter, however, had held on and took his first race win for Ferrari.

In Monaco, Scheckter took pole position and drove to a relatively easy win after Villeneuve dropped out with transmission problems – along with several other front-runners. At that point, with Scheckter strengthening his hand in the title race, the team told Villeneuve that he would now be expected to support Scheckter's title bid wherever possible. Then came the French Grand Prix and the cementing of the Villeneuve legend.

In its third season of Formula 1, Renault needed to show something for its experimental turbo car programme, and its prime focus was on victory at the sweeping Dijon circuit. Thus the yellow cars swept the front row of the grid, but it was Villeneuve who got off the line fastest to lead the way. He held out until lap 47, when his Michelins were going off the boil and Jabouille drove past, then the second Renault of René Arnoux began to close in as the final laps ticked down.

On lap 78 of 80 Arnoux got past Villeneuve;

ABOVE Villeneuve blasts off, Long Beach 1979. *(Schlegelmilch/Getty)*

BELOW The Ferrari 'train' hits Monaco. *(Sutton)*

but then the Renault's engine began to splutter and Villeneuve pushed his way back ahead. Throughout the last lap of the race the pair indulged in as wild a battle as Formula 1 has ever known, passing and repassing one another, banging wheels and slithering on and off the track. At the final corner Arnoux drifted a little wide and Villeneuve was able to go down the inside and the two crossed the line just two-tenths of a second apart. Renault had won its first race but all that anyone cared about was Villeneuve's battle to hold on to second.

The two Ferrari drivers were now first and second in the title race, eight points apart. The British Grand Prix at Silverstone was next on the agenda and this is where the team was at its most exposed. The British teams may not have had their own track like Fiorano but most were based close to Silverstone and spent day after day pounding around the bleak old airfield honing their ground-effect cars.

With their Michelin tyres not enjoying the Northamptonshire asphalt, Scheckter and Villeneuve qualified 11th and 13th respectively and played no major part in proceedings, which ended with Clay Regazzoni scoring the first Formula 1 win for Frank Williams' eponymous team. In the next three races – Germany, Austria and Holland – Williams triumphed each time, with team leader Alan Jones taking the honours each time.

In his wake the Ferraris struggled – Scheckter scoring two fourth places and one second place, Villeneuve one second place, one eighth place and his celebrated retirement at the Dutch Grand Prix. After passing the dominant Williams of Alan Jones around the outside of the looping Tarzan bend, Villeneuve's left rear tyre burst, pitching him off the track. He restarted the car, reversed out of the catch fencing and set off on three wheels at unabated speed. So fast, in fact, that he tore the left rear corner off completely.

BELOW **Fast, sweeping Silverstone was a bump in the road for Ferrari.** *(Sutton)*

LEFT ***'Ciao, campeone!'*** **Scheckter savours the spoils at Monza.** *(Sutton)*

That race dropped Villeneuve to fourth in the points. Scheckter remained on top and his title could be confirmed if he could just win the Italian Grand Prix at Monza with Villeneuve in second place. That is exactly the order in which they finished – just 0.4 seconds apart – after Villeneuve dutifully held to his agreement and rode shotgun to his friend all the way to the finish line.

With the championship settled and the pressure removed, Villeneuve was let off the leash in the last two races in North America. At home in Montréal, the Villeneuve myth was continued when he pulled out a lap two seconds faster than Scheckter to qualify on the front row. He led for 50 laps before his Michelins gave out and allowed Alan Jones through for yet another win – although every time the Australian reined in his pace a fraction, Villeneuve would be there, sliding luridly, in his mirrors.

At Watkins Glen for the US Grand Prix, Villeneuve underlined the legend when Friday's practice was held in a violent downpour. He went out and attacked the track, stating that if the race was going to be that wet it was better to be prepared, and skittered his aquaplaning T4 around the circuit 11 seconds faster than Scheckter in second place on the timesheets. He qualified third in dry conditions, but it rained again on race day and, after dealing with Jones' Williams, he won by a 50-second margin despite having to slow down and nurse an engine with falling oil pressure.

The Ferrari 312T5 and the 1980 season

The winter of 1979–80 was a time of relative serenity at Ferrari, with no major changes in the driver line-up or its management structure. Forghieri, however, was hard at work with the rest of his technical team in trying to conjure up a new 1.5-litre turbocharged engine. It was clear that the 312 engine had just about reached the end of its extended lifespan, that aerodynamics were crucial as never before and that Williams now had the car to beat.

The engine was less important now than aerodynamic purity. This was anathema to Ferrari's way of going racing. Forghieri turned his attention to the prodigious power that might be unlocked from a turbocharged engine while the 1980 car, the 312T5, was only a mildly reworked T4.

The chassis was updated in order for it to be able to house the new turbo engine for testing purposes but in racing trim it would be powered by the final iteration of the Type 015 V12. It had seemed reasonable to believe that the

ABOVE **Lightning reactions saw Villeneuve hoist the 312T5 higher than it deserved to be.** *(LAT)*

title-winning car from 1979 could still compete strongly in 1980. Yet the season was to be an unmitigated disaster.

Scheckter soon realised just how bad the situation was and, with one eye on retirement and the other on his 1979 championship trophy, was already thinking of new business opportunities to pursue in 1981. He scored two points all season long.

For Villeneuve such thoughts were tantamount to treason. He had hoped to win the title in 1980 but was left wrestling an unwieldy beast of a car that was using Michelin tyres now designed solely for the benefit of Renault's turbo machine – but despite his disappointment he could not restrain himself and hammered his cars to the limit of his own prodigious gifts.

There were some great performances from Villeneuve, such as his charge to sixth place in the German and Dutch Grands Prix. Probably the two finest drives of the Canadian's stellar career were spent achieving fifth place in Monaco – in driving rain on slick tyres – and another fifth place at home in Montréal where he had started 22nd on the grid.

But there were also a worrying number of accidents in 1980. The car simply could not do everything that Villeneuve asked of it and when things broke he allowed himself little or no margin. A heavy crash in Argentina was followed by a narrow escape in Brazil. Worst of all was an enormous accident in the Italian Grand Prix at Imola that saw him sitting, stunned, in the wreckage of his T5, completely robbed of vision by the violence of the crash.

The story of the brilliant 312T series therefore ends on an unbecoming footnote – but for five seasons it had won the richest of rewards for those talented men who created it and drove it at the pinnacle of the sport.

ABOVE A lonely road for Villeneuve, doing battle with the unloved 312T5. *(Sutton)*

LEFT Williams assumed dominance in 1980 with Ferrari left reeling. *(Sutton)*

MICHELIN
5
ellesse
Agip
BROOKLYN
BROOKLYN
JODY

Chapter Two

Anatomy of the Ferrari 312T series

In designing the Ferrari 312T, Mauro Forghieri blended innovation – a successful transverse gearbox – with a chassis and engine that resounded with the great tradition of building racing cars in Emilia Romagna. In the course of six years and seven variants the achievements of Forghieri's 312T series would become legendary.

OPPOSITE Jody Scheckter sits calmly in the pits while the team does its work. By modern standards he is exposed to many perils, but the 312T4 was supremely competitive. *(Schlegelmilch/Getty)*

RIGHT **Forghieri's brilliance matched well with Ferrari's traditional values.** *(Schlegelmilch/Getty)*

The 312T series itself divides into two sub-series. First come the pre-ground-effect cars of 1975–78, the 312T–T3. Next come the closest thing to ground-effect cars that could be built while using the wide V12 engine, the 312T4–T5.

None of the engineers at Ferrari, not even Forghieri himself, had the luxury of experimentation that was afforded to the likes of Len Terry at Tyrrell, Gordon Murray at Brabham or Peter Wright at Lotus. The British-based teams revelled in devising new concepts within the framework of the regulations – if not always within their intended spirit – that was never part of the psychology at the Scuderia.

In part this was due to the nature of Forghieri's horizontally-opposed V12 engine, which for a decade gave the cars from Maranello an abundance of power that required no innovative aerodynamics or weight-saving technology to challenge for victory. But it was also a reflection of Enzo Ferrari's abhorrence of new engineering techniques that he deemed to be 'faddish' when his own experience was rooted in the comforts of the past.

When John Cooper began winning Grands Prix with cars that placed the engine behind the driver, Ferrari had scoffed that one should not put the cart before the ox. He had eventually recanted, but long remained true to his belief that a strong engine and a determined driver should make the difference between success and failure. Aerodynamics was not an art form that he ever troubled himself with unduly.

These were the areas of Forghieri's concern, although Ferrari trusted and respected his chief engineer as much as any man, it still often required considerable argument from Forghieri and the sporting management for consent to be granted to try new technologies while the sport evolved around them.

Specification

Ferrari 312T

Initial car designed in 1974 and taking part in the 1975 season through to the first three races of 1976.

Ferrari 312T2

First variant, with slightly increased wheelbase and replacement of overhead airbox with 'nostrils' on either side of the cockpit in line with new regulations. In the winter of 1975–76 a de Dion rear suspension was tested but not raced. For 1977 mild aerodynamic upgrades were made to the bodywork and several new front and rear wing designs were deployed. The T2 raced on into the first two races of 1978 using an upgraded engine, Michelin radial tyres and revised suspension.

Ferrari 312T3

The first major changes to the fundamental 312T chassis, including a larger central fuel tank behind the driver and redesigned front suspension sitting against the outside of the chassis in order to work better with the new Michelin tyres. New, more angular bodywork deleted the 'nostril' ducts on the front of the car in favour of more effective sidepod tunnels and use of chimneys to extract hot air on top of the sidepods – a feature that would not become commonplace until the late 1990s. A narrower front track was tried and used with success at the British Grand Prix, which gained favour with the later specifications of Michelin tyres. From late in the 1978 season experiments with sliding skirts and generating downforce through ground effect were conducted but the T3 was never a ground-effect car.

Ferrari 312T4

The first true ground-effect car built in Maranello, using the foundations of the T3 but with a new chassis designated 022 and designed to be as narrow as possible to enable better airflow beneath it, with the fuel tanks becoming centralised and the sidepods and ancillaries mounted on outriggers. Greatly increased usage of aluminium honeycomb bolstered the strength and rigidity of the tub, pushing it closer to being a full monocoque. Two large panels formed the floor of the car, which had a lip like a keel running from the nose section to the front of the engine – a lighter and more powerful variation of the Type 015 V12 engine. New, flatter bodywork designed to generate maximum downforce was employed after a strenuous development programme involving significant wind-tunnel work in partnership with both Pininfarina and Fiat.

Ferrari 312T5

Broadly similar to the T4 but with revised suspension and updated aerodynamics. The technical team's focus and budget for 1980 was placed squarely upon developing a new 1.5-litre V6 turbo engine. Anything else was secondary, which is a primary reason for the team's catastrophic fall from grace.

Ferrari 312T6

A six-wheel test hack built in 1977 using Ferrari 312T2 chassis 025. The T6 was fitted with de Dion rear suspension that had been tried on a standard T2 but shelved. It was fitted with two standard front wheels, with four more of the same front wheels attached in pairs at the rear to replace the standard rear wheels. The car exceeded the maximum width restriction and was never intended to race.

Ferrari 312T8

A publicity stunt that attempted to wrong-foot the British teams who were experimenting with six-wheeled concepts, a photograph was created using the T2 in which two pairs of standard front wheels were apparently mounted at the front, like the Tyrrell P34, and two pairs of standard rear wheels were mounted at the rear. The resulting 'eight-wheeler' image was then leaked to the press. No such car ever existed.

Chassis

In 1973–74 Mauro Forghieri's reworked 312B3 reduced the polar moment of inertia – its physical bulk – by centralising the weight of the car and throwing it as far forwards as possible. The 312T was to be the next step, bringing all the mass of the transmission forward of the rear axle.

The chassis that was to house this new powertrain needed to be lightweight, adjustable and easy to repair, which is why Forghieri abandoned the fully stressed skin of the 312B3 in favour of a traditional tubular steel frame on to which panels of sheet aluminium and aluminium honeycomb were riveted.

'Our type of chassis was, in comparison with the others, a little heavier but with the same rigidity,' the great designer remembered. 'One benefit was that it was easier to repair even when outside the factory. In 1963–64 we had started using monocoque construction but there was no great difference to the rigidity until the ones made from carbon fibre [the 126C3 in 1983].'

BELOW The solid-looking structure of the first 312T kept all weight low down. *(Author)*

Tony Matthews's superb cutaway of a Ferrari 312T. *(Tony Matthews)*

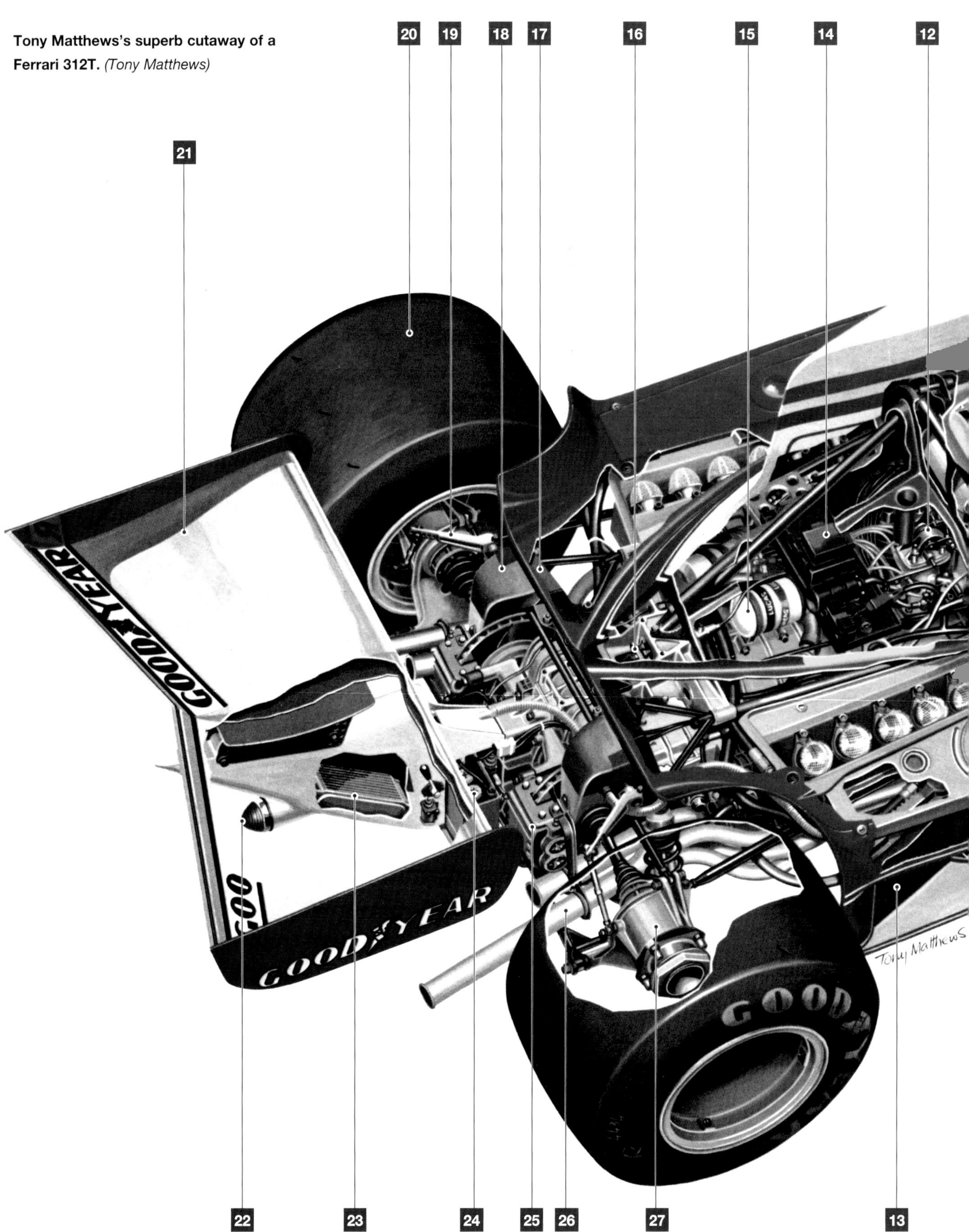

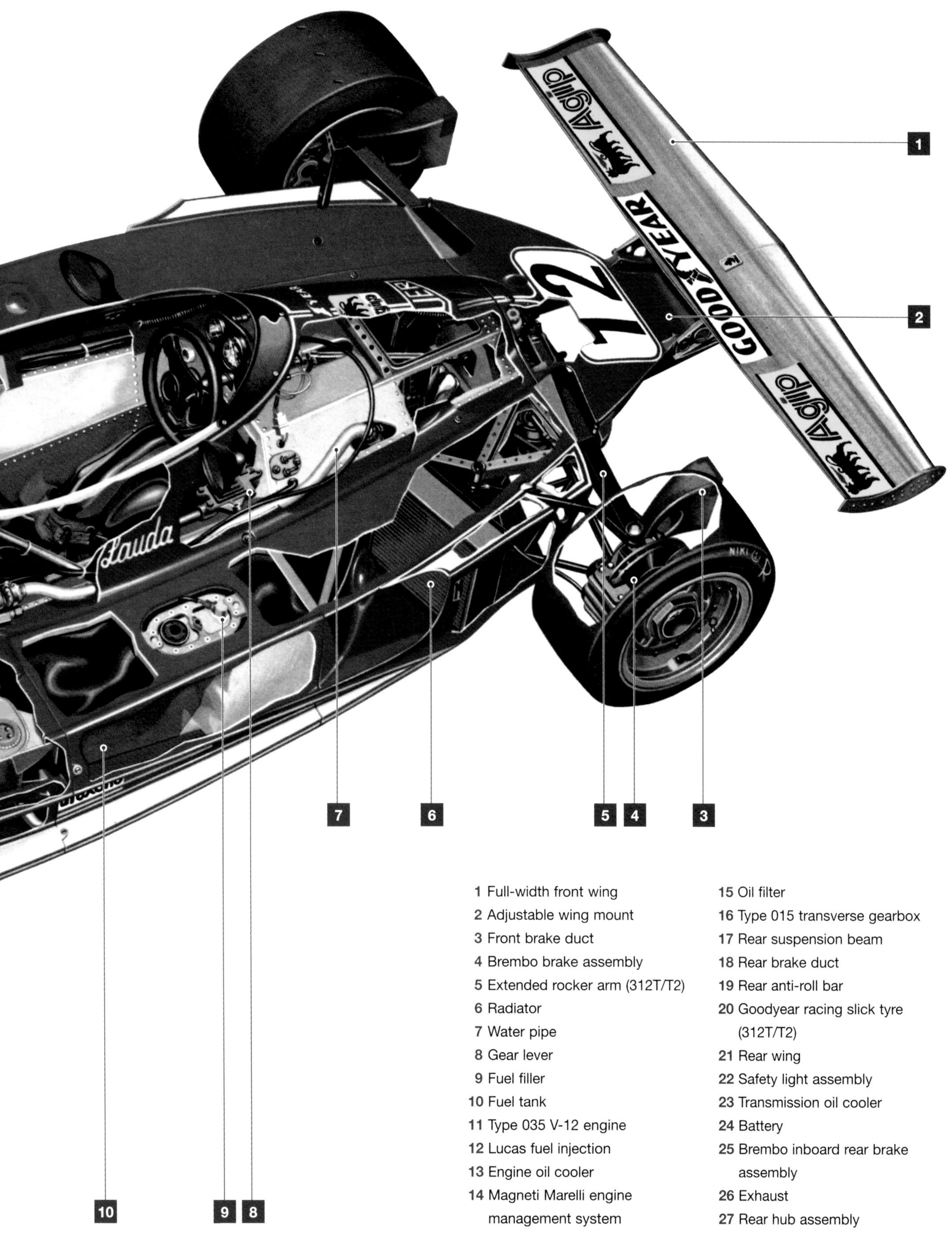

1 Full-width front wing
2 Adjustable wing mount
3 Front brake duct
4 Brembo brake assembly
5 Extended rocker arm (312T/T2)
6 Radiator
7 Water pipe
8 Gear lever
9 Fuel filler
10 Fuel tank
11 Type 035 V-12 engine
12 Lucas fuel injection
13 Engine oil cooler
14 Magneti Marelli engine management system
15 Oil filter
16 Type 015 transverse gearbox
17 Rear suspension beam
18 Rear brake duct
19 Rear anti-roll bar
20 Goodyear racing slick tyre (312T/T2)
21 Rear wing
22 Safety light assembly
23 Transmission oil cooler
24 Battery
25 Brembo inboard rear brake assembly
26 Exhaust
27 Rear hub assembly

RIGHT By 1979, the need to save weight and create airflow made a very different beast. *(LAT)*

BELOW Clever ducting and low centre of gravity are apparent once the bodywork is removed. *(Author)*

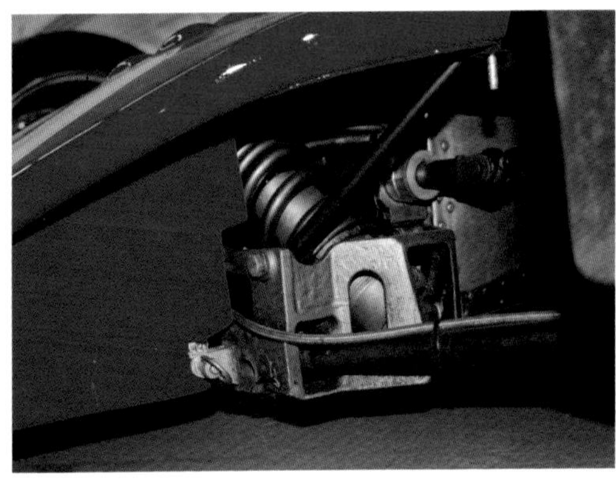

RIGHT Detachable castings designed to protect the chassis in the event of an 'off'. *(Author)*

The basic framework at the heart of the car was formed of box tubing welded together between steel bulkheads to the front and rear. The aluminium panels were then drilled, countersunk and riveted in place, triangulated to resist bending and torsional loads. Lines of rivets would therefore trace the basic framework on to the exterior skin of the car, which could be seen to clearest effect on cars such as the 312T4 in the pit lane with their bodywork removed.

In sectional form, the shape of the 312T chassis was hexagonal at the rear bulkhead and quadrilateral at the front bulkhead, tapering inwards from top to bottom. Inside the cockpit, the pedals sat immediately behind this front bulkhead.

In the earlier 312T and T2, the riveted skin would only reach up as far as the waistline of the car – in fact with the one-piece bodywork removed only the driver's torso, the roll hoops and steering wheel stood proud of the top of the sidepods. In comparison the later cars appear much more robust, cladding the central fuel tank and reinforcing the torsional stiffness of the chassis to the point where the chassis of the T4 and T5 wore what appeared to be a suit of armour that reached from the floor to the top of the roll hoop.

Whether it is the 'barely there' chassis of a 1975 312T or the 'end-of-the-line' 312T5, the design and construction of the chassis does not fundamentally differ. The devil is in the detail, however, and what really makes the skeleton of the 312T series stand out from its contemporaries is in Ferrari's expertise in making lightweight alloy castings.

'There was no aircraft industry in Italy as such so there was no major advance in chassis technology, but the craftsmanship that went into the castings was incredible,' said historic racing expert Rob Hall, who has refurbished and race-prepared almost every design of the era. 'What stands out with the Ferrari is that you get lots of little sub-castings at the front that take all of the spring mounts and so on, and that meant that in an accident you would more likely break the casting but save the chassis.

'Perhaps Ferrari, by retaining the traditional chassis, was always going to be heavier than a monocoque but the reasoning behind it was very clear. To keep the weight down there was more use of lighter alloys in the construction, but Ferrari would have had more budget to work with on that front than a privateer British team that had a customer engine and a much smaller budget but plenty of bright ideas.'

The radiators and fuel tanks are then fitted on to the outside of the arrow-like core of the 312T series structure, becoming integral parts of the overall chassis and giving the Ferraris their distinctive manta ray-like plan form compared to the arrow-shaped layout of contemporaries like the McLaren M23 and Lotus 77.

In no small part this is due to the FIA requirement, from 1973 onwards, to place 'a crushable structure' between the more breakable parts of the car, such as the driver and fuel tank, and the outside world. Whereas the British teams elected to keep the radiators largely exposed in a delta shape in front of the rear wheels, Forghieri fitted the Ferrari's radiators deep inside the curvaceous bodywork and allowed them to 'breathe' through comparatively ornate-looking 'gills' that were cut out to allow cooling air in and hot air out.

'They're quite substantial when you get them off, and the top deck is one piece and then there are all these ducts and passages built into them and foam for impact protection, so while the car looks wide and substantial there's not much mass there,' said Rob Hall.

At the front of the sidepod sat the water radiators, one on each side. The water pipes from the engine to the radiator run along the top of the chassis on each side of the cockpit opening, hidden inside bodywork when the car is buttoned up ready for action. A sunken duct cut into the cockpit surround kept a supply of cooling air passing over the radiators, while the hot air was expelled up and out through the large ducts located near the driver's elbows.

Engine oil radiators are located at the rear of the sidepods, alongside the engine and just ahead of the rear wheels. They are seated lengthways within the bodywork to keep their weight low and angled outwards, front to back, in order to scoop as much cool air as possible through the mesh. The oil tank was placed just in front of the right-hand radiator, the oil filter next to the left-hand radiator.

ABOVE Forghieri eschewed the wedge in favour of a flatter, forward-weighted layout. *(Author)*

LEFT Water cools at the front of all 312T series sidepods. *(Author)*

LEFT Plenty of cooling needed for the big V12 – carried by substantial pipes. *(Author)*

LEFT Oil stays close to home on all 312Ts. *(Author)*

ABOVE Drivers sat between the main fuel tanks on the 312T and T2. *(Author)*

LEFT The later cars needed sidepods to create downforce, moving fuel behind the driver. *(Bonhams)*

One key feature is the placement of cut-outs in the bodywork that enable mechanics to quickly check the oil level mid-pit stop without undue fuss – a unique feature of the Ferrari that illustrates that it has brains as well as beauty.

Between and behind the front-mounted water radiators and rear-mounted oil radiators lay the three fuel tanks. This is common to all the 312T series, although in the 1975–77 cars the central tank was very discreetly located down around the driver's coccyx, with much larger tanks to either side of him. Increasing amounts of aluminium honeycomb were bonded to the designs in line with the level of downforce being generated by the cars, to the point where the much narrower T4–T5 chassis is almost a full monocoque once again.

'The T5 is still a great car but they're clearly trying out different ideas and the engine isn't bolted in and the fuel tank goes in behind the driver rather than down the sides and it's altogether more conventional,' said Rob Hall, 'detail changes that were compromises to try and get the underfloor area as clear of ancillaries as possible.'

CENTRE Elegant simplicity: the 1975 312T made it all look very easy and logical. *(Author)*

LEFT Square, wide and handsome: the 312T3 marked the first fundamental rethink. *(Bonhams)*

LEFT **The 312T4 looked like the combination of a shark, a wheelbarrow and a science experiment.** *(Bonhams)*

Aerodynamics

The science of aerodynamics was not a subject towards which Enzo Ferrari felt particular warmth. His belief was that engines won races in the hands of the right driver. Yet the emergence of wedge-shaped cars from Lotus – the 72, 76 and 56 gas-turbine car in particular – caught Mauro Forghieri's attention.

In 1972 he built a new wedge-shaped body for the 312B2 which took the Lotus wedge several steps further down the line, placing the radiators down the car's flanks and reducing the frontal area as much as humanly possible, cutting giant ducts into the front wing to feed them. The result was an angular freak that earned the nickname *Spazzaneve*, or 'Snowplough'.

After the false start of Colombo's 312B3, Forghieri returned and brought with him greater refinement to the basic *Spazzaneve* concept. He applied it to the revised B3 of 1974 and refined it into its definitive, curvaceous form on the 312T.

The fundamental aerodynamic shape of the early 312T series was led by reducing frontal area and ensuring that the mass of the car sat between the front and rear axles. Using the shape of the car to generate downforce was considerably further down the list of priorities.

The job of generating downforce fell primarily to the large alloy aerofoils: the full-width trapezoidal wing mounted above the

BELOW **Where it all began: Forghieri's radical 312B2 *Spazzaneve* concept of 1972–73.** *(LAT)*

BOTTOM **The 312T had a lot going on but made it all seem fairly effortless.** *(Author)*

RIGHT Full-width front wing would be present on all 312T models from 1975–80. *(Author)*

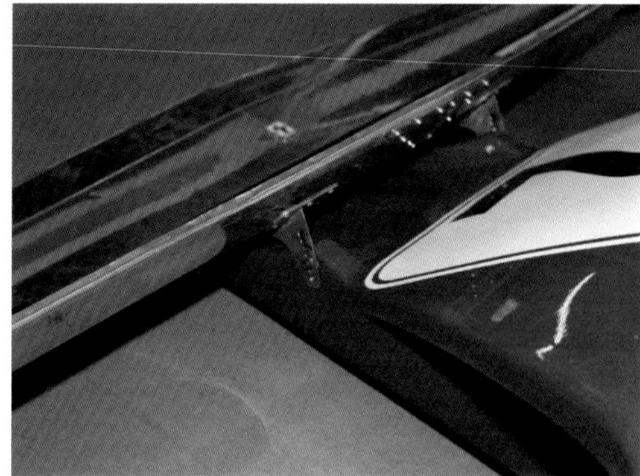

FAR RIGHT Substantial and adaptable mounting made adjustments easy. *(Author)*

FAR RIGHT Revisions on 312T3 placed the wing further out from a narrower nose. *(Author)*

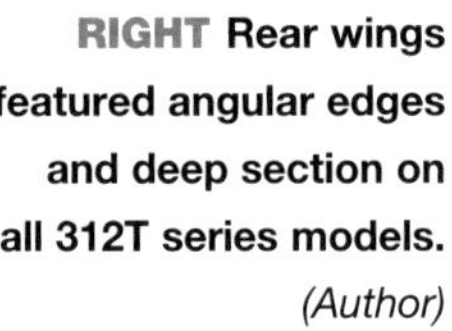

RIGHT Rear wings featured angular edges and deep section on all 312T series models. *(Author)*

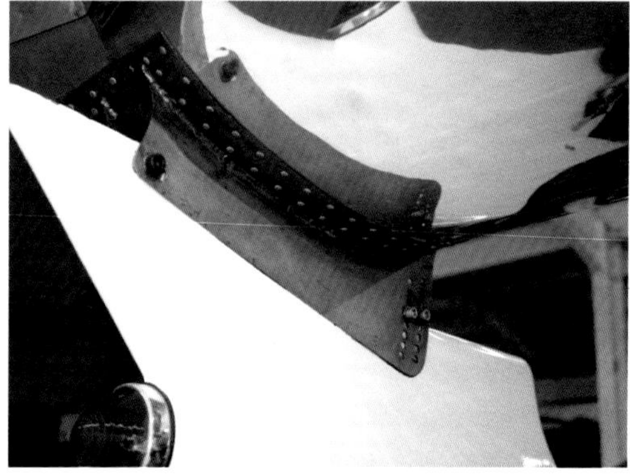

FAR RIGHT Ease of adjustment was a priority to the rear just as it was to the front. *(Author)*

RIGHT The first major revision was the 312T3 tail assembly, featuring pivot mounting. *(Bonhams)*

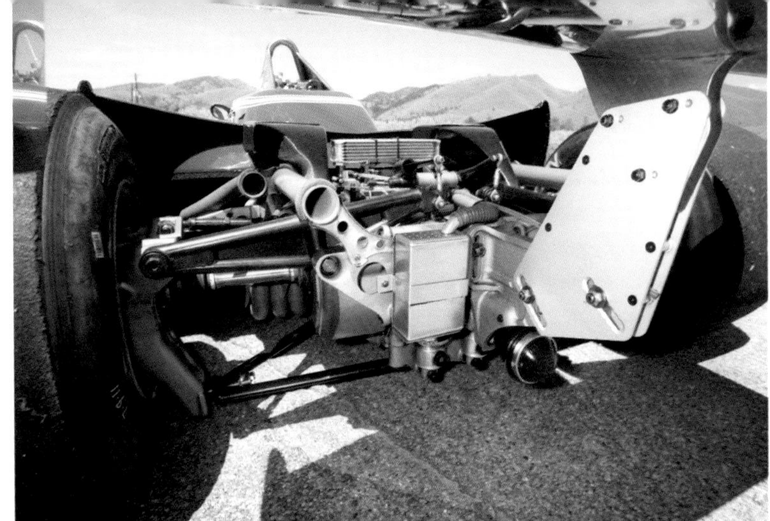

RIGHT Solid and substantial fitting on the 312T4 and T5. *(Bonhams)*

nosecone and the high-mounted rear wing with a deep cross-section. Both the front and rear wings were robust designs that were easily – and almost infinitely – adjustable to suit the track and were amongst the most effective in the field, generating around 330–350kg of downward thrust for most circuits.

The other areas of the car to be influenced by the airflow were the air intakes for the engine, the brake cooling ducts and the wheels – the habitual problem for open-wheel cars. Ferrari attempted to minimise the aerodynamic effect of the front wheels by fitting shrouds around the high-pressure area, but these were quickly abandoned when it became clear that they upset the airflow around the car more than they helped it – although similar shrouds were incorporated into the rear of the sidepod around the rear wheels of the T1 and T2.

The relative innocence of aerodynamics is shown by the way that the car's aerodynamics are all focused upon how the 312T managed the air that it was driving into, with virtually no consideration for the potential of the air expelled behind and underneath it to improve performance. The bodywork just stops in line with the rear axle and the air passing underneath the car was allowed to slow and disperse at random around the mechanical parts of the car in a way that the arrival of ground effect would render hopelessly inefficient.

ABOVE When the 312T2 was revealed, shrouds on the front wheels attempted to stabilise airflow. *(LAT)*

BELOW LEFT Flick-ups carried air around the tyres – although slowing its passage to the rear wing. *(Author)*

BELOW Like all F1 designs, balancing the needs of cooling and generating grip is paramount. *(Author)*

RIGHT Rear heat exchangers were of particularly risky placement, catching only a fraction of passing air. *(Author)*

BELOW Sidepod 'funnels' were a novelty in 1978 but the norm 20 years later. *(LAT)*

BELOW Without funnels at Brands Hatch, Reutemann's winning car shows the cleaner lines of 312T3. *(Bonhams)*

Recent computer simulations studying the 312T have shown that Forghieri's integrated system of slits and tunnels to feed cold air and remove hot air from the radiators was risky. The surface of the heat exchanger barely saw any cold air at all tucked away in line with the direction of travel, and although its layout has since become standard in Formula 1 the surface area has grown and vents and louvres have been placed to feed them.

The original aerodynamic package of the 312T as it was revealed in late 1974 changed little for the next three years. In order to keep pace with the British teams, who were closing the gap with their latest chassis, Mauro Forghieri and his team kept chipping away at fine-tuning the design, developing specific aerodynamic packages for specific circuits and updating the suspension and rear bodywork, but fundamentally the first real change came with the 312T3 of 1978.

At first glance the 312T3 retained many hallmarks from its predecessors but was packaged in a more angular manner. Its wings remained full-width trapezoid designs at the front and high-mounted at the rear but the 312T3 showed a much greater understanding of aerodynamics as well as Forghieri's first tentative exploration of the influence that air passing beneath the car had to offer.

The T3 benefitted from much cleaner upper bodywork with none of the vents of its predecessors. A sign of the growing sophistication was the almost complete removal of the aerodynamic shrouds around the rear wheels, which caused more problems than they solved by creating a low-pressure area in front of the rear wing and reduced its capacity to generate downforce. Instead two narrow 'funnels' appeared in front of the rear wings to disperse hot air from the radiators – a feature

that was to become common currency some 20 years later.

The reason why the upper surfaces of the 312T3 were so much cleaner was that all the air intakes were mounted below the waistline, scooping in vast quantities of air from behind the front wheels and directing it through a series of tunnels that not only fed the radiators but also caused the air to speed up as it passed through the car. Ground effect was making its way into the 312T series make-up.

'We had no permission to use skirts in 1978,' Mauro Forghieri recalled. 'Mr Ferrari did not permit their use because, in his opinion, they were outside the rules. Remember how the skirt was born? – in 1977 Lotus had permission from the commission to use a fixed broom; the rest copied them without permission.'

With significant investment of time and money in wind-tunnel work at Pininfarina, Forghieri re-imagined the ultimate aerodynamic package of the 312T4 for 1979. The upper surface was now completely cleared of unproductive lumps, bumps and vents, tilting up gradually behind the cockpit where the air was channelled back towards the rear wing by triangular fins that helped maintain the shape of the air and complete the seal around the car.

All of the fuel tanks were mounted centrally behind the driver, throwing the cockpit forwards when compared with the earlier T series cars and helping to give the distinctive manta ray appearance to the front end. Inexplicably the rear bodywork still stopped abruptly in line with the rear axle, leaving the engine and transmission exposed to wreak havoc on the airflow as it passed behind the car and beneath the rear wing.

Both the front and rear wings remained of outwardly similar construction and styling to their pre-ground-effect predecessors, but by now they were merely contributing to the overall levels of downforce rather than being solely responsible for it.

The sidepods, now mounted on outriggers, were a much more central part of the airflow from front to rear. Bigger, more effective ducts fed the heat exchangers and controlled the speed of the air and its effect upon generating grip through the new underbody floor panels. These in turn were still some way short of the

TOP By the end of the 1978 season, Forghieri's experiments with semi-skirts were evident – if not approved of by the founder. *(Powell/Getty)*

ABOVE While British teams made their bodywork all-enveloping to generate downforce, Ferrari kept its mechanical parts exposed. *(Bonhams)*

BELOW Air passing within the bodywork of the 312T4 had plenty of work to do. *(Bonhams)*

ABOVE The working environment of the 312T3. *(Bonhams)*

BELOW Weight savings were to be found everywhere for 1979 – making the cockpit a much less substantial environment. *(Bonhams)*

full-blown venturi to be found on the Lotus 79 and Williams FW07, due not only to the breadth of the horizontally-opposed V12 but also oversights such as the splayed exhausts – which would finally be re-routed out of the airflow at Monza for the title-deciding Italian Grand Prix.

Cockpit

In order to make life easier for the drivers, the one-piece bodywork that was common to all 312T series models was often removed to enable ingress and egress from the cockpit. The driver slipped down snugly into his seat to see a broadly similar view in all five iterations of the type, albeit with certain key changes in the rest of his environment over time.

Immediately in front of him was mounted a small, thick-rimmed steering wheel with an ignition cutout switch on one of the spokes. The short, stubby gear lever sat ready for the driver's right hand, just in front of the bulkhead atop Ferrari's dog-leg gate which gave a very clear-cut and positive movement throughout the five forward gears, with reverse sitting in the sixth slot behind a foolproof metal gate. The industrial-strength gear linkage sat exposed beneath the selector, running below the driver's elbow back towards the gearbox.

On the left-hand side of the bulkhead sat the fuel pump switch and starter button, above which the fuses sat readily accessible in case of need. On the early cars, the 312T and 312T2, the hoses connecting the front-mounted water radiators to the engine ran over the top of the

RIGHT The fabled Ferrari gear selector remained virtually unchanged throughout the 312T series' career. *(Author)*

FAR RIGHT Water hoses flanked the cockpit on 312T and T2. *(Author)*

ABOVE Simple, clear and functional layout on 312T. *(Author)*

ABOVE RIGHT Lightweight alloy pedals completed the driver's world. *(Author)*

RIGHT Steering and suspension all fit neatly around the driver. *(Colin Bach collection)*

chassis on either side of the cockpit, faired in beneath the cockpit cowling when the car was ready to take to the track.

Directly in front of the driver, behind the steering wheel, was mounted the triangular fascia within the forward rollover hoop. Just three gauges were to be found here, dominated by the large, centrally mounted tachometer that indicated engine rpm, calibrated from 4,000 to 14,000 in 100rpm increments with numbers at every thousand. To the right sat the combined oil pressure and fuel gauge, to the left the water temperature gauge. As per almost all Ferraris, the gauges were made by Veglia Borletti.

In the 312T and T2 the driver sat flanked by the large alloy faces of the fuel tanks as though reclining in a bath of 102 octane. In the 312T3 and T4/5 the side radiators were eliminated and mounted behind the driver up to head level, bringing his feet even closer to the scene of an accident – all the more so as the front suspension had been moved from the front of the chassis to either side of the footwell.

'It's like a piece of jewellery really, which is typical for a Forghieri Ferrari of the time,' said Rob Hall. 'The gear change is unique and it's a well-thought-out car, and when you sit in it you feel the privilege of being able to drive it. It's a bit special.'

LEFT Removable casting and canted-over shock absorbers defined the early 312T series. *(Author)*

Suspension

The suspension of the Ferrari 312T series was one of the most inventive and effective elements of the design, giving the cars very distinct handling that allowed their drivers to make the best use of Forghieri's low polar moment of inertia and extremely low centre of gravity.

The 312T did not corner like other cars and neither Lauda nor Regazzoni would corner in the sort of tail-out drift that thrilled the crowds

RIGHT The long arm of the early front suspension had to be a substantial piece. *(Author)*

FAR RIGHT The front anti-roll bar was actuated by a series of links and levers. *(Author)*

RIGHT Reversed lower wishbones replaced the parallel link suspension of the earlier 312B series. *(Author)*

FAR RIGHT Anti-roll bar maintains order in traditional fashion. *(Author)*

and correspondents in equal measure. With a 48/52 weight distribution, the cars could be driven through corners with similar cornering forces being generated front and rear, all of which was sprung using a unique set-up.

The front suspension utilised double wishbones and was activated by very long fabricated steel rocker arms compressing Koni coil spring/damper units mounted inboard on their own alloy casting, which also contained the anti-roll bar.

The springs and dampers were mounted at an angle, almost touching at the top and reaching the full width of the chassis at the bottom, in order to reduce the car's frontal area. A more conventional approach was adopted at the rear, which used reversed lower wishbones with an upper arm activating outboard Koni springs and dampers with a central radius arm that was fitted with an anti-roll bar.

This fundamental arrangement of the suspension was carried over to the 312T2, which introduced a fractionally longer wheelbase. 'It was done to improve the stability in constant high-speed corners,' said Mauro Forghieri. 'Changes from 312T to T2 brought less movement in roll at 2.5G–3G with the same tyres.'

The T2 was to serve the Scuderia well for the 1976 and 1977 seasons but, by the time that Niki Lauda wrapped up the 1977 World Championship title, a brave new world beckoned with Michelin's radial tyres that would require a major rethink of the car's suspension.

The result was the 312T3, which saw Forghieri adopt a much more conventional front suspension layout in which much shorter tubular rocker arms operated a much sturdier pair of spring/damper units that were moved to sit in a more traditional upright position on castings flush with the outside wall of the pedal box. This was the preferred set-up for the Michelin radial tyres.

The 312T3's rear suspension retained transverse links and radius arms with the spring/damper units placed outboard. In an experimental set-up the anti-roll bars at the front and rear were connected by levers to induce anti-dive and anti-squat measures, but the system did not work as hoped.

The T3 laid the groundwork for Forghieri's first attempt to bring ground effect into the mix with the 312T4. The resulting car would be fractionally heavier, significantly more powerful and generate significantly more downforce than its predecessors.

BELOW LEFT Beam mounting holds the top half of the suspension in place atop the transverse gearbox. *(Author)*

BELOW By 1978 few major changes had taken place, although the mounting points were now integral. *(Bonhams)*

ABOVE **Longer, lighter and less metalwork was involved in holding the rear of the 312T4 and T5 together.** *(Bonhams)*

BELOW **Rear brake assembly: inboard and air-cooled from ducts that were retained throughout 312T series.** *(Author)*

RIGHT **Prominent front brake ducts are synonymous with the 312T series.** *(Author)*

FAR RIGHT **Rear brake ducts are more discreet but effective.** *(Author)*

At the rear, the 312T4 utilised Koni's rear spring/damper units mounted inboard and inside their own aerodynamic tunnels. The front suspension retained the fundamentals of the T3 with tubular rocker arms operating a much sturdier pair of spring/damper units that were moved even closer to the driver's feet. Following the experimental set-up of 1978, the T4 had front and rear anti-roll bars that were successfully connected using hydraulic rather than mechanical means for effective anti-dive and anti-squat measures to maintain the ground-effect vacuum beneath the car. This set-up would be carried through to the T5 in 1980, while Forghieri and his team focused upon bringing the new turbo engine project to life.

Brakes

Throughout the Ferrari 312T series of cars, the brakes followed the same layout: the front brakes were located outboard and the rear brakes inboard in order to reach Forghieri's optimum weight distribution.

BELOW **Air-cooled Brembo brakes delivered a big step for Ferrari in 1975.** *(Author)*

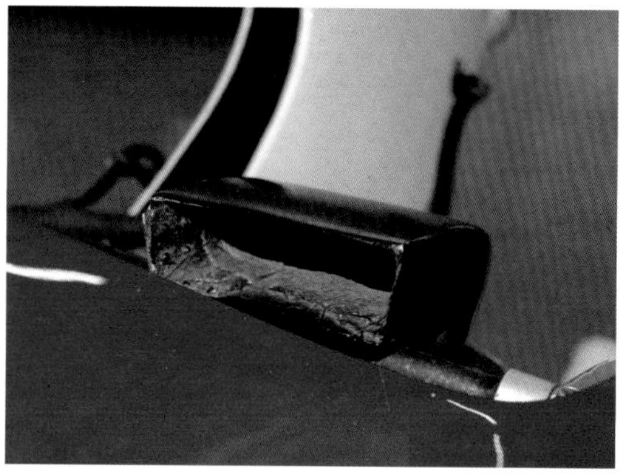

LEFT Modern tyres are all Avon-made for historic racing. *(Author)*

In 1975 the 312T marked the introduction of Italian braking specialist Brembo to the Formula 1 arena, bringing its ventilated cast iron discs that were mated to Lockheed calipers. On the early 312T and T2 the most obvious components of the braking system were the fibreglass ducts that fed air to the centre of the hub, from where it was dispersed through the drilled disc.

The ducts themselves were dispensed with as Brembo brought out newer and more heat efficient iterations of its braking systems, ridding the cars of a significant cause of drag and disturbance in the airflow.

Wheels and tyres

The wheels on the Ferrari 312T series remained constant in style throughout the 1975–80 seasons, being of lightweight cast alloy with four-spoke front wheels and largely featureless deep dish rear wheels that featured a ribbed finish on the inside of the rim. The front hubs were mounted on very large diameter ball races on hollow stub axles. All wheels were located by pegs and retained by very large single nuts, tightened with a pneumatically driven socket spanner.

In 1975–76 Goodyear held a complete monopoly on Formula 1 tyre supply, allowing it to continue supplying the sport with slicks and wets of cross-ply construction which, aside from their dimensions, were little altered from tyres of a decade before. In 1977 Michelin entered the fray and brought with it radial technology that had been proven in testing with Scuderia Ferrari. Renault's ambitious new team had exclusive rights to use the Michelin tyres in its debut season of 1977, but Ferrari negotiated a supply deal commencing at the start of 1978.

Today in historic racing Avon is the only approved supplier, using its approved A11 compound rubber.

FAR LEFT 'Rifled' finish on the 312T series deep-dish rear wheels. *(Author)*

LEFT Front wheels retained a four-spoke design from 1975 to 1980. *(Author)*

MICHELIN

Although its tyre technology had been used to win the very first Grand Prix in 1906, French tyre giant Michelin did not officially join the ranks of Formula 1 tyre suppliers until 1977. When it did finally make the leap, Michelin brought with it an innovation that had never been tried by the likes of previous suppliers Continental, Goodyear, Engelbert, Dunlop, Firestone or Pirelli: radial-ply tyre technology.

By 1977, radial tyres had long-since replaced those of traditional cross-ply construction for road car use but they had not yet been used in Formula 1, where Goodyear had held a monopoly on supply.

Traditional cross-ply or bias tyres were constructed with layers of textile cords that overlapped and were then coated with rubber. The different angles to the direction of travel at which the ply overlapped within the tyre gave it specific properties, allowing the tyre's performance to be tailored fairly precisely, but they were slightly inflexible and this was shown to be a handicap.

In comparison, Michelin's radial tyres were made from ply cords that were set horizontally across the direction of travel and braced by a steel or textile band that was moulded into the rubber.

Testing had proven that Michelin's radial tyres offered less distortion under load, with more flexible sidewalls that helped to maintain the contact patch under acceleration and braking and withstand much higher cornering forces. Braking and traction increase as a result, slip angles are reduced on cornering, steering response is sharpened, lateral stability is improved and tread wear slashed. Not only that but the radials also proved to have better stability in a straight line, giving drivers more confidence at high speed.

Ferrari was well aware of the potential that the radial tyres had. 'We had been testing Michelin tyres since 1971, maybe,' Mauro Forghieri recalled. 'They had a strong influence on suspension movement, camber and turn-in variation, and also on aerodynamic behaviour and suspension philosophy.'

By 1976 Michelin's competition tyres manager, Pierre Dupasquier, had convinced everyone up to the level of François Michelin and his board of directors that the time was ripe to tackle the world's biggest motorsport series with Ferrari. Michelin agreed to enter Formula 1, but it would be impossible to start out with Ferrari because Renault was preparing to enter its radical new 1.5-litre turbocharged F1 effort, and as a *Régie d'Etat* (state-owned company) it would be unconscionable for Renault to go racing on anything other than French tyres.

In 1977 it was clear that, whatever the frailties of Renault's new turbocharged power unit may have been, the Michelin tyres were potentially brilliant.

Pierre Dupasquier was summoned to Maranello, where he was ushered into the presence of Enzo Ferrari who asked how he could get Michelin to provide its tyres for his cars. Dupasquier replied that Michelin was working with Renault because it had an Original Equipment Manufacture supply relationship with the French manufacturer to provide tyres for its road-going products. Very quickly Michelin

RIGHT Michelin and Ferrari were close before entering F1 together – even closer afterwards. *(Sutton)*

LEFT Michelin tyre development was fast and effective, relying upon driver feedback. *(LAT)*

became an OEM supply partner of both Ferrari and its parent, Fiat, and a new contract to supply its radial Formula 1 tyres to the Scuderia from 1978 followed soon afterwards.

The 1978 season would see Michelin's engineers working closely with Mauro Forghieri and the experienced Scuderia Ferrari staff. In the course of 16 races, Michelin identified that the three key areas that would influence tyre performance were the grain of the asphalt at each track (how much space there was between the pieces of gravel), the type of gravel used in the asphalt (smooth or abrasive) and the temperatures that the track surface could be expected to run at in the course of a race.

These variables were found to be the major influences on tyre distortion and therefore tyre performance. The optimum tyre compound to maintain the correct surface tension between the rubber and the road would then be chosen based upon these measurements, and a map of the World Championship circuits was developed to show which were the least 'severe' in terms of tension, such as Brands Hatch, to the most difficult to manage, such as Interlagos.

An increased sensitivity to wheel camber remained a disadvantage but that could be managed through changes to suspension geometry – something that Forghieri pre-empted by moving all the suspension components outside the tub for ease of access.

Acting more as a technical partner than a traditional supplier, Michelin brought an army of technicians and a raft of different tyre solutions to try and optimise performance. At one test in the winter of 1979–80, for example, it brought 40 different compounds to be assessed for any additional latitude that could be found in the tyres' ideal operating temperatures. It is no overstatement to say that the modern science of tyre management can be traced back to Michelin's campaign of the late 1970s.

The process was not without frustrations and Michelin found life to be rather more demanding with Ferrari – which was in contention for the 1978 World Championship for the majority of the season – than it had been with just the struggling Renault effort.

One significant flashpoint came at the British Grand Prix, when Dupasquier was summoned to Forghieri's motorhome. Team leader Carlos Reutemann had wrestled his 312T3 up to eighth in qualifying but was struggling for grip and deeply unhappy with the car. He was falling away from the title race and, in Dupasquier's telling of the story, Forghieri let it be known in no uncertain terms that he believed Michelin was at fault.

'For a quarter of an hour, Mauro explained to me that our tyres didn't stand up in comparison with the Goodyears, that our rate of progress was too slow, that we were bad engineers and lots more "kind things" of that sort. I just took notes and when I thought he had finished I said, "I understand, Mauro. Ferrari is a team that wants to win the World Championship and can't waste its time with a team such as you have just described. The next Grand Prix will be in Germany in a fortnight and I believe you must get in touch with Goodyear immediately."'

Fortunately for all concerned, the two parties reconciled fairly quickly. Late on the Saturday evening new tyres arrived from France, S76 compound and higher-profile by 4cm at the front, 3cm at the rear, while Forghieri and his team set about fitting the Argentinean's preferred narrow front track to the 312T3. On race day Reutemann started strongly, profited from some retirements and eventually hounded down the leader, Niki Lauda, to secure what the great Argentine described as his finest win.

The reserves of knowledge gained and shared between Ferrari and Michelin continued to grow throughout the second half of the season and the intensive winter of testing in 1978–79 ultimately delivered the package with which Scuderia Ferrari would claim the last World Championship titles of the 312T series' career.

ABOVE Forghieri's horizontally opposed V12 retained its fundamental architecture for nearly a decade. *(Bonhams)*

RIGHT The V12 requires 50% more of everything compared to a Cosworth DFV – a packaging challenge. *(Author)*

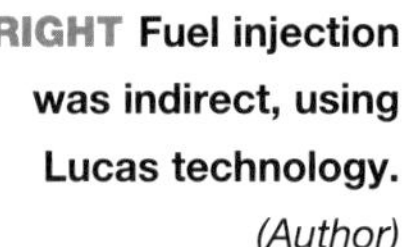

RIGHT Fuel injection was indirect, using Lucas technology. *(Author)*

RIGHT Wiring the V12 is an art form in itself. *(Author)*

Engine

Although commonly referred to as the 'flat-12' or 'boxer' engine, the Type 015 powerplant of the 312T series, a development of the engine that made its debut in the 312B of 1970, was no such thing.

A true boxer has one crank pin per piston, while in the 180° V-engine, two opposing pistons share the same crank pin – this in turn influences the shape of the crank and the ignition sequence; a boxer engine's opposing pistons move towards each other while a V-configured engine's pistons move in unison. It was the latter which was the configuration of Forghieri's celebrated screamer.

When it was launched in 1970, the engine boasted around 470hp. By the time that the 312T was unleashed in 1975 it was closer to 490hp and by the time that the 312T series ended it was up to a thumping 520hp – which is a lot in any car, all the more so a car with such a relatively short footprint and a weight-forward bias.

'It was a bit brutal, depending on the track, and suffered from inaccurate set-up, but the 12-cylinder was progressive, much more than the 8-cylinder,' said Mauro Forghieri. 'There were many changes to the engine in the first 18 months. We got 20hp more than it had given on the test bed.'

This was, of course, significantly more power than the Cosworth V8, and Ferrari's 12-cylinder was also more efficient than the other 12-cylinder engines of Alfa Romeo, BRM and Matra that appeared and faded away in the lifespan of the 312T series. Cosworth found new ways to wring more power from its engines, which kept Ferrari on its toes due to the weight and workload of its components, as historic preparation specialist Rob Hall explained:

'On a V12 the spark box, the dynamo and things like that use 50% more energy all the time – whether that's fuel or electrics – so you have to stay on top of that. Batteries need to be in top condition. They run higher fuel pressure so the pump has to be able to deliver 50% more than it would on a DFV. A DFV is 120psi and with a V12 you really need 140psi. That's meaning that the components are being used that little bit harder.'

Throughout the competition history of the Type 015, Forghieri's team sought to reduce the weight and increase the available power – and they achieved this with no loss in reliability. It was the unburstable nature of the powerplant that contributed as much to Jody Scheckter's title win as his Michelin tyres or the much better aerodynamic package of the T4.

One often-overlooked element in achieving greater performance from the engine is in the fuels used. Italian petrochemical giant Agip stepped in to partner the Scuderia in 1974 after its original partner Shell, which had been one of the first investors in Enzo Ferrari's outfit as far back as 1929, withdrew its programme in the wake of the OPEC crisis of 1973. By 1975, the technical support available from Agip was at the sort of level that Ferrari needed.

'We were very happy with both fuel and oil,' Forghieri remembered. 'They were a very efficient research group. I remember their study on engine combustion in function of tumble and swirls, and the use of water in gasoline to reduce the knocks.'

The first step change in the Type 015 engine came in 1976 with the introduction of the 312T2. Ferrari's rivals had lobbied successfully for the abolishment of high airboxes, ostensibly on the grounds of safety but also believing in several quarters that it would rob the V12 of a valuable boost in power through the 'ram air' effect of its high-mounted scoop. In fact, the resulting 312T2 had more power again thanks to an uprated compression ration which, Forghieri asserted, 'mainly improved efficiency and widened the torque band, which was so important for me and the drivers.'

Fundamentally the architecture of the Type 015 changed very little between 1975 and 1980 but its construction did, as Ferrari fell back on its unrivalled expertise in casting alloys to reduce weight in the engine's construction.

'As the cars evolved there's more magnesium used on the engine like all the front covers, the sumps ... they started off with those in aluminium but with each year they would save weight by casting more and more in lighter alloys like magnesium,' said Rob Hall. 'It's a bit like when the Cosworth DFV first came out: it didn't have as much power as the rival engines but they kept developing it. The Ferrari had

ABOVE The alternator was mounted directly behind the driver on the 312T of 1975. *(Author)*

LEFT Agip took over from Shell as Ferrari fuel and oil supplier in 1974 and would remain until 1996. *(Sutton)*

LEFT Magnetti Marelli provided the brain of the beast on all 312T series engines. *(Author)*

RIGHT Clutch return spring and detail on the casing of the transverse unit. *(Author)*

RIGHT Water from the front radiators was piped into the casing. *(Author)*

BELOW The remarkably compact rear assembly was home to exceptional power and torque. *(Author)*

ample power but mass and weight problems were always factors with the V12s.'

The increased titanium and magnesium content of the engines was mirrored by refinements to the internals of the engines year-on-year. 'It was different mainly from the continuous improvement of every part of the heads, ducts and combustion,' Mauro Forghieri said.

The Type 015 was also a load-bearing unit like its great rival from Cosworth. However, to shore up this larger engine a pontoon structure was built over the top to clamp it firmly in place and reduce the risk of unwanted damage from vibration.

However, the bespoke approach to building these engines plays against the Type 015 in historic competition, when confronted with an array of Cosworth-powered cars that have been developed at a fairly breathless pace.

'Unfortunately for the fans the Ferraris aren't used as much as the Cosworth cars, as in fact the DFV is still in development and getting more power now than it did when it was new,' Rob Hall confirmed. 'With the Ferrari engines, when you are repairing them, servicing them or keeping them running, you tend to see them in the hands of collectors rather than racers so it's really a matter of keeping them running rather than keeping them competitive.

'Running them is no more difficult but they are a bit more tricky to get parts for. You have to make more parts, which increases the lead time you need, whereas I could get all the parts to build a fresh DFV tomorrow.'

Gearbox

The very fact that the Ferrari 312T series gained its name from the transverse layout of its transmission says a great deal about its importance. And yet for all that the notion of making a more compact unit by laying the gears across the direction of travel was not an altogether new idea.

Although it is thought of as being a largely conventional customer car, the 1954 Maserati 250F placed its bevel gears on the input side and the final drive through spur gears to make an effective transverse unit. As fine a handling car has never been built, but the transverse gears did not take off as a concept in F1 – although many empires were built sideways in the road car industry – and it was not until 1972 that the next transverse 'box would appear.

This was the March 721X, which used a transverse Alfa-Romeo sports car gearbox mounted between the tub and the engine. The

LEFT The 312T transverse gearbox was indelibly stamped on F1 history. *(Author)*

BELOW Throwing weight forward defied conventional wedge aerodynamics and layout, delivering supple handling. *(Author)*

RIGHT **Compact and bordering on chunky: what the 312T's rivals saw of it in 1975.** *(Author)*

idea was to have the weight centred as much as possible, to give the car a low polar moment of inertia, which would make it more responsive. It failed dismally and nearly ended the career of Niki Lauda – which is why he was less than thrilled when, in a battle for the 1974 World Championship, he heard that Mauro Forghieri was planning a transverse unit for 1975.

'The new transmission was already on paper in 1973,' Forghieri said. 'The new 312B3 was the result of the heavy testing work done in winter 1973–74. The result convinced me about the new ideas for the forthcoming "T". Walter Salvarani was the designer responsible for the gearbox and, for me, he was one of the best.'

While Forghieri and Salvarani were at work on the 'box itself, Borg & Beck was called in to develop a clutch and differential capable of managing the new set-up. As Mauro Forghieri pointed out, Ferrari had been using a limited slip differential since 1966 but the new layout would provide its suppliers with headaches of their own to resolve.

Adding to the complexities, the 312T transmission required its own oiling system with a cooler incorporated in the support for the rear wing. Nevertheless, the system was tested to destruction at Fiorano in the winter of 1974–75 and by the time that the new car made its debut the gearbox was as rock solid as the rest of the design.

Just like the engine, the transmission was continuously upgraded and lightened throughout the next six seasons. 'The gearbox was used to mount the rear suspension so when they changed the suspension they had to change the casting of the gearbox and evolve it that way,' said Rob Hall.

'There was clearly a lot of thinking on the hoof – mechanics would doubtless say "that's hard work, can't we make it easier?" and the later gearboxes are much more user-friendly from that point of view. You can hear the conversations in the pit garage: "Why did we miss most of that practice session?" If the answer is that the gearbox takes longer to take apart and work on than it should then there's an incentive to change it, and clearly Ferrari did that through the years.'

The first change to the cars came in 1976, in line with the uprated engine in the 312T2. 'Lighter gears for less weight and friction,' Mauro Forghieri explained. This was to be the longest-serving iteration of the gearbox, but from it the lessons learned were put into a completely redesigned unit for 1979, to be mated to the lighter and more powerful V12 engine.

By that stage, Forghieri and his team had also tried out a new invention: a semi-automatic transmission. The intention was, as its successful antecedents would prove, to deliver as close to seamless a shift as possible that minimised the potential for human error and any damage to the powertrain that might result. Cutting the time to change gear to hundredths of a second may have seemed like science fiction in 1978–79 but the advantages of such a system were obvious.

'The semi-automatic gearbox was a normal manual one operated by an hydraulic system with oil pressure pumps and an electric magnetic device controlled by the rpm of the engine,' Mauro Forghieri confirmed. Sadly, this was too much of a stretch for even Ferrari's technical resources at the time, as attested by Peter Windsor's visit to a test session in 1979 when Villeneuve managed just a couple of laps.

Indeed, when a semi-automatic transmission was finally debuted by the Scuderia in 1989 it was the cause of considerable friction between John Barnard's team in Guildford, Surrey, which had designed it and the engineers in Maranello who had to maintain it. Many who were there – including the Scuderia's future tactical doyen Luca Baldisserri – believed that it was too early even in 1989 for such a system to be in front-line service … which highlights the forward thinking going on back in 1978–79.

LEFT Transmission fluid routed in tidily. *(Author)*

LEFT Later gearboxes evolved to be lighter and cannot be interchanged. *(Bonhams)*

'The engines and gearboxes are pretty much bespoke to each car from the T to the T5 because things like the suspension mountings were bespoke,' Rob Hall concluded. 'They were designed to do a job – winning the World Championship – and so the changes in designing and building them were focused on that completely.'

LEFT Ferrari would return to semi-automatic transmissions a decade later – bringing success and a good measure of pain to achieve reliability. *(LAT)*

Chapter Three

The Ferrari 312T drivers

The men who climbed aboard the 312T series of cars were heroes. They were also in that elite group who did not just drive for Ferrari: they drove for Enzo Ferrari. Each of them had to have the required spirit to stand tall in front of a man who had managed Tazio Nuvolari and Achille Varzi, who had created the legend of the *Cavallino Rampante* and whose passion for racing had outlasted both the bombast of Mussolini and the rancour of the Vatican.

OPPOSITE **The men who drove the Ferrari 312T defined the word 'hero' for millions around the world.** *(Bob Harmeyer/Getty)*

Even when hidden behind his trademark sunglasses, those hooded eyes could eviscerate lesser souls and thus demanded that his drivers were men who were out of the ordinary even among the stellar talent and inherent bravery on display in Formula 1 in the 1970s. Every one of them was.

Clay Regazzoni

Two grand prix wins with Ferrari 312T.

Swedish author Per-Olof Enqvist once said: 'One day we shall die. But all the other days we shall be alive.' These are words that would have resonated with Gianclaudio 'Clay' Regazzoni, the roguish racer who personified the early days of the 312T series and seized each day to wring the most speed and enjoyment from it.

The Swiss driver was a darling of the *Tifosi* and this was a love affair that ran both ways. His first stint at Ferrari began in 1970, when he finished fourth on his debut and won the Italian Grand Prix at Monza to trigger euphoria for a 'home' win (Regazzoni hailing from Switzerland's Italian-speaking region of Ticino).

He was gregarious and fitted right in to the swashbuckling stereotype of drivers of that era. When a beautiful young student decided to streak the whole length of an Alitalia jumbo jet flying to Johannesburg, there was little surprise among the Ferrari men on board that the one item of clothing she wore was Regazzoni's race helmet. It was just one among legions of such incidents whenever 'Regga' was around.

Regazzoni's first stint at Maranello was cut short by shifting political sands at the end of 1972. He was nevertheless drawn back into the fold for 1974 by the lure of a new, more straightforward team structure being built under Luca di Montezemolo. Not only that but Regazzoni convinced Enzo Ferrari that his young Austrian team-mate, Niki Lauda, was a youngster who could go far – despite an unpromising record at that time. Indeed, the decision to hire Lauda was inspired but it is often forgotten that Regazzoni held the upper hand at Ferrari in 1974. Although he won only once, at the Nürburgring, and claimed just one pole position, Regazzoni's consistency saw him finish just three points shy of title winner Emerson Fittipaldi at the end of the year while Lauda, with two wins and eight pole positions, ended the year 14 points further back.

That was to be Regazzoni's greatest season. By 1975 Lauda had fully assumed leadership of the team and, despite taking a euphoric victory

RIGHT
Clay Regazzoni.
(Sutton)

ABOVE
Niki Lauda.
(Schlegelmilch/Getty)

at the Italian Grand Prix, Regazzoni's stock was falling. By 1976 he was on his way out of Maranello for the second and final time.

Niki Lauda

Seven wins in the Ferrari 312T. Six wins with the Ferrari 312T2. World Champion in 1975 with the Ferrari 312T and 1977 with the Ferrari 312T2 (also World Champion in 1984 with McLaren).

Andreas Nikolaus Lauda is a man of seemingly endless contradictions. He treated motor racing as a clinical exercise yet defied the last rites to make his return to the cockpit just six weeks after his near-fatal accident in 1976. He was a precise analyst of performance yet quit the sport in 1979 because he claimed that the sound of his Brabham's Ford Cosworth V8 did not inspire him in the way that the wailing 12-cylinders of BRM, Ferrari and Alfa Romeo had done before. He acted as a consultant to the movie *Rush*, which dramatised his accident and the 1976 championship battle with James Hunt, only to release his own documentary, *Lauda: The Untold Story*, in cinemas soon afterwards.

Enzo Ferrari was left unimpressed by 'the little Austrian' at their first meeting – during which Lauda had appeared unwilling to make eye contact, according to Ferrari's right-hand man, Franco Gozzi. When he first drove the Ferrari 312B3 at Fiorano, Lauda stated that it was 'shit', despite being implored to exercise a little diplomacy by Piero Lardi Ferrari, who was translating for his father.

After providing Mauro Forghieri and his team with the required insights to fine-tune the Ferrari 312B4 into a winner during 1974, Lauda's raw speed was made abundantly clear – although his impetuosity cost him vital championship points. He returned for 1975 stronger both mentally and physically, dedicating himself to becoming the fittest driver in the paddock, and mated the brilliant but brutal speed of the Ferrari 312T with a silky smooth driving style and brilliant tactical awareness that delivered a crushing first World Championship title.

According to Gozzi, this ascetic style of racing still sat uneasily with Enzo Ferrari, who bemoaned the fact that his star drove 'like an accountant'. Despite such occasional outbursts of petulance, however, even Ferrari himself must have admitted that, through Lauda, the Scuderia had been plucked from the brink. The Austrian's prickly temperament and methodical approach had not been seen since Ferrari's last World Champion, John Surtees, way back in 1964.

It is a source of frustration to many that, 40 years on, the Lauda legend is defined by his burnt face and a title fight with James Hunt that was only made possible by the Nürburgring crash that so scarred him. His achievements were far more profound and far-reaching than that, and were the product of a brilliant – if sometimes explosive – partnership with Mauro Forghieri. The wilful and passionate Italian designer gained unfettered access to the analytical Austrian's immense ability to provide feedback.

Lauda won the 1977 Drivers' World Championship but his relationship with Ferrari had become untenable. The Scuderia had never defended Lauda against the hysterical Italian press when they accused him of cowardice for pulling out of the title-deciding Japanese Grand Prix in 1976, and had not been slow in signing first Carlos Reutemann and then Gilles Villeneuve as potential replacements. With his second World Championship victory secure and two races remaining on the calendar, Lauda walked away from Maranello without a backward glance.

BELOW **Carlos Reutemann.** *(LAT)*

Carlos Reutemann

Two wins in the Ferrari 312T2. Three wins in the Ferrari 312T3.

There is no greater contrast between the eras than when one looks at the baby-faced stars of modern Formula 1 and then back at an archive shot of Carlos Reutemann in his prime. The Argentinean star's features were those of a matinee idol – albeit one whose career depended upon him staring into the abyss every time he climbed into the cockpit. He had an aura of impending tragedy about him.

The prevailing opinion among those who were there is that Reutemann was too sensitive to be World Champion. He was a man who had survived the most vicious years of death and injury in the sport and yet lacked the killer instinct required to blot all of the possible consequences out of his mind. He was sublimely fast and arrived at Ferrari as a proven race winner with Bernie Ecclestone's Brabham team, but was also tremendously insecure at times and spent the first 18 months of his tenure at Maranello at the heart of a bitter war between Ferrari and its star driver, Niki Lauda.

Reutemann was convinced to break with Ecclestone in the summer of 1976 when Lauda's very survival, let alone his return to competitive action, appeared to be in doubt. Yet when the negotiations ended, Reutemann arrived in Monza for his first race as a Ferrari driver only to find that he was to be given a third car at Ferrari, alongside Clay Regazzoni and the returning figure of Lauda. He was then put on the substitute's bench for the rest of the year.

Regazzoni was dropped for 1977 and Reutemann, buoyed by Ferrari's support, finished third in Argentina and won in Brazil – taking the championship lead while Lauda struggled to get into a rhythm. Yet he was unable to dominate the Austrian, who fought back through consistency on the track and superior political skill to take the title with two races remaining.

In 1978 Lauda was gone and Reutemann, paired with the wild young Canadian rookie Gilles Villeneuve, was able to enjoy life out of the Austrian's shadow. Nevertheless, this was also the time when the Lotus ground-effect cars were at their apex and Ferrari had increasingly little opposition to offer the black and gold steamroller of Mario Andretti and Ronnie Peterson. Peterson's death in the Italian Grand Prix made what looked like the most competitive seat in the sport come available and Lotus wanted Reutemann to fill it. He went – and was beaten to the 1979 World Championship by Jody Scheckter's Ferrari.

Gilles Villeneuve

One win in the Ferrari 312T3. Three wins in the Ferrari 312T4.

Enzo Ferrari's definition of the perfect racing driver was based upon the wiry little Mantuan maestro, Tazio Nuvolari, who illuminated Grand Prix racing in the 1930s. Nuvolari would race every lap as if it was his last; would race with broken bones encased in plaster; would race simply for the joy of racing. After 40 years of searching, Enzo Ferrari finally found his successor to Nuvolari's indomitable spirit in the form of Gilles Villeneuve.

At the 1977 British Grand Prix, Villeneuve's debut with McLaren astonished onlookers by spinning the car numerous times in practice as he reversed the usual logic and worked back from the speed that he wanted to reach to the speed of which the car was capable. Already the legend was practically writing itself…

Moving to Ferrari, Villeneuve's wild ways were not universally popular. His reputation as a lead-footed rock ape persisted in certain quarters of both the press and the paddock, which meant that victory, when it came, was cathartic. On the Île Notre-Dame circuit in Montréal, racing in front of his fellow *Québécois*, Villeneuve gently protected his soft tyres on a full fuel load and then began hunting the leader, Jean-Pierre Jarier, when the Frenchman's Lotus sprang a leak and promoted the first – and so far only – Canadian winner of the Canadian Grand Prix.

Three more wins followed in 1979 and a title challenge that was only stymied by Villeneuve's natural ebullience. His wheel-banging battle with René Arnoux to claim second place in France brought censure but sealed his legend. Driving to the pits on three wheels at barely checked speed at Zandvoort reinforced both Villeneuve's hero status and criticism of his balls-out approach to racing. Meanwhile, away from the limelight, Jody Scheckter was also racking up victories that were backed up with the solid points finishes that would eventually see him claim the World Championship title.

At the start of the 1980 season Villeneuve justifiably believed that he could be champion. A paltry six points was scant reward for his unflagging self-belief and spectacular racecraft in the face of overwhelming superiority granted to the ground-effect cars of Williams and Brabham and the power of the turbocharged Renaults.

ABOVE
Gilles and Joann Villeneuve. *(LAT)*

RIGHT **Jody Scheckter.** *(Bob Thomas/Getty)*

As it turned out, that mercurial 1979 season would prove to be Villeneuve's one and only chance to take the title. Even if most of the points lost that year were from self-inflicted problems on the track, it is impossible to believe that Villeneuve would ever have changed his style one iota – and for that he is still revered.

Jody Scheckter

Three wins in the Ferrari 312T4. World Champion in 1979.

By the time that he joined Ferrari, Jody Scheckter had spent just six seasons in Formula 1 – but that was sufficient to turn the wild child of 1973 into a hard-bitten professional. They say that pessimists are disappointed optimists, and in Scheckter it was true to say that he was a veteran hardened by the constant threat of death that stalked the era.

As a youngster, the South African had lived in the moment and drove the wheels off every car that he climbed aboard. Bitter experience – such as arriving at the scene of François Cevert's catastrophic accident at Watkins Glen in 1973 – saw him fashion a prickly demeanour that kept most people at arm's length while he honed a more calculating approach to racing.

Formula 1 was a business – one at which he excelled and thus commanded considerable seniority in the paddock, matched by an unprecedented salary of $1.3 million plus prize money when he signed with Ferrari for 1979.

On the track, Scheckter was well worth the money, but he did little to further the Ferrari myth in the way that his Tigger-ish young team-mate Gilles Villeneuve did. Scheckter left the romance to his colleague and instead set about the job of bringing home the championship with single-minded determination. At least posterity allowed Scheckter to claim his title on the hallowed ground of Monza before an outpouring of delirium from the TIfosi, who would have to wait 21 years for another champion.

Perhaps irked by Scheckter's apparent indifference to his mythology, there was no official word of congratulation from Enzo Ferrari until the team returned to Maranello, when a simple '*Ciao, Campeone!*' was the proffered greeting.

Having scaled the heights of the sport, Scheckter struggled to summon the motivation needed to wrestle the lame duck 312T5 in 1980.

His love affair with racing was long-since over, and at the end of the year he simply turned his back on the job and invested his moderate fortune into developing far greater wealth from training Americans how to use firearms. It was to prove a very shrewd move indeed.

And the other Ferrari 312T driver...

In the mid-1970s, Giancarlo Minardi was a young man building his reputation as a team boss in Formula Italia under the banner of Scuderia del Passatore. This became Scuderia Everest, in deference to sponsorship from an industrial rubber company. Minardi's driver was Giancarlo Martini, a month older than Minardi, who carried the team up to Formula 2 before an agreement was signed with Ferrari to act as its driver development operation.

The idea was that Scuderia Everest would prepare Formula 2 cars using the Dino 246 engine and run the most promising young Italian drivers in non-championship Formula 1 races in a year-old 312T.

Scuderia Everest duly arrived at Brands Hatch in mid-March equipped with Ferrari 312T chassis 021 that had been prepared for Giancarlo Martini to drive in the *Daily Mail* Race of Champions. Martini qualified second to last and managed to crash on the warm-up lap. A month later, at the International Trophy at Silverstone, Martini was similarly out of his depth and the Scuderia Everest F1 team, the last privateer Ferrari to appear in a Formula 1 race, was quietly forgotten.

Minardi remained in Formula 2, initially running Ferrari engines, and eventually established himself as a Formula 1 constructor in 1985. At the wheel was another Martini – Giancarlo's nephew, Pierluigi, who would go on to score Minardi's first-ever World Championship point in 1988, lead one lap of the 1989 Portuguese Grand Prix and start from the front row of the 1990 US Grand Prix.

BELOW
Giancarlo Martini.
(Sutton)

GOODYEAR
GOODYEAR
Agip
HEUER
12
Agip
GOODYEAR

Chapter Four

The team

In the 1970s, Scuderia Ferrari was in many ways a different place to the large corporation that now resides in Maranello. It is an era and a group of people who are as steeped in myth as the cars that they created – and they were even at the time that they were racing. Like any successful legend, it was always very much founded upon fact.

OPPOSITE **The class '75. World Championship winners for the first time in more than a decade, Scuderia Ferrari drivers and staff gather around the 312T.** *(Sutton)*

ABOVE Master of all he surveyed: Enzo Ferrari holds court in Maranello. *(Mondanori/Getty)*

Wherever you were in the world during the 1970s, there were journalists reporting back with tales of a unique team behind those impossibly glamorous scarlet racing cars. A team that was fiercely Italian, capable of mixing bonhomie and seriousness in equal measure, staffed by mechanics who might just as easily burst into song as scowl at a prying photographer.

At the epicentre of that myth was the man who conjured it: Enzo Ferrari. Viewed from afar he seemed a remote, omnipotent figure but, in Maranello, the Scuderia was undeniably a close-knit organisation and it was ruled with an iron fist by *l'Ingegnere* (the Engineer), as Enzo Ferrari wished to be described.

This was a title which gave him a sense of belonging among his employees, having little truck with either the title of *Commendatore* bestowed upon him before World War Two or his drivers' insouciant description of 'the Old Man' – although he probably quite enjoyed the reputation he had around the factory as *il Drake* (the Dragon).

Ferrari was not, of course, an engineer. His brilliance lay elsewhere in a role he once described as being 'an agitator of men'.

As much as it would probably pain Ferrari to hear it, there is much in the way that Bernie Ecclestone today carries himself through his ninth decade that has echoes of *l'Ingegnere* at the same stage in his life. There is a shared sense of mischief and theatre from men who have long since mastered the art of having the world hang on their every utterance.

While the engineers and team staff built and prepared the cars, Enzo Ferrari wove the legend of the Scuderia before his audience's very eyes, such as when Niki Lauda witnessed his employer giving an interview in which he was asked how he viewed himself and the company he had built up.

'When I look into the mirror in the morning even I don't understand myself,' he sighed, much to Lauda's keen enjoyment, which was doubled when *l'Ingegnere* added: 'Some things in life are truly inexplicable.'

For all his theatricality, the respect and awe in which his staff held him was no illusion. In his interviews for this book, even a man such as Mauro Forghieri, who was responsible for so much of the genius behind the 312T and its successes, defers to his late patron on key issues.

When asked, for example, whether discarding Ferrari's long-standing success in the World Sportscar Championship at the end of 1973 was bittersweet, he replied: 'The decision was taken by Enzo Ferrari alone. F1 was more important for everybody…'

That view is one shared by Pietro Corradini, one of the race engineers for whom life became much less cluttered under the new F1-focused regime at Maranello. 'I think that period in the early seventies was difficult for Ferrari because we were too few people divided between F1, the last of the big engine prototypes, the 512 S and 512 M, plus the new 312PB prototype for the smaller engine.'

One of the constants in Maranello throughout this time of change was Enzo Ferrari's personal assistant, Brenda Vernor, an Englishwoman who had arrived in Maranello as the girlfriend of one of Ferrari's key drivers of the 1960s, Mike Parkes. She would recall the ways in which, behind the theatre, *l'Ingegnere*'s passion for what was important for everybody in Maranello could be manifested.

'If a member of the family, a mechanic or somebody, had a problem financially or they needed a specialist and there was a six months' waiting list, they'd go and ask him and he'd phone up and make an appointment and sometimes even say, "No, I don't want any money." He'd pay for it.'

This paternal attitude towards his employees helped Ferrari to maintain a unique bond within the team – a sense of family, complete with squabbles and all. As someone at the heart of the operation, that is exactly what Brenda Vernor remembered.

'When the guys were preparing the cars for a race, I used to go down there late at night, to take them Lambrusco and a cake or panini and sit with them,' she recalled fondly. 'You couldn't do that now. Now there's a guardhouse. It's like trying to get into Alcatraz.'

Such a close-knit community and such a degree of veneration for the head of that family did not sit easily with all those who were part of the 312T series story. The wry amusement that the Scuderia caused to its matter-of-fact 1979 World Champion, Jody Scheckter, remains tangible even after more than 35 years.

LEFT In all team affairs, *l'Ingegnere* had the final word, and even Forghieri deferred. *(Sutton)*

ABOVE Jody Scheckter brought a no-nonsense approach to the team that few drivers equalled. *(Sutton)*

'I remember people telling me, you know, [that] I'm the grumpy small bear and I'll never get on with people at Ferrari,' he recalled. 'I actually had a great time, you know? I really had a great time. I suppose I gave them as much BS as they gave me and the food was a massive improvement from the white sandwiches and pickles in the English teams! I had a great time there, really.'

Men like Scheckter could get the job done but there was always some wariness among the team's long-serving staff about the way that they chose to address *l'Ingegnere* – particularly when it came to perceived shortcomings in their machinery. Quite often they found themselves moderating conversations between their employer and the men who drove his beloved machines, as Scheckter soon found out.

'You wouldn't want to insult the car or anything like that,' he remembered. 'We came back from Argentina after the first race and there were engineers around and he said, "What do you think? What do you think?" I said: "The engine hasn't got the power" – because the Fords were pulling out of the corners quicker than us – but they wouldn't translate. I said "No, but..." but they wouldn't translate it because they knew there would be such trouble because he loved his engine.'

Such diplomacy was not a particular concern to the other man to win the World Championship in a 312T: Niki Lauda. Unlike Scheckter, who was able to remain attuned to the sensibilities of those around him, Lauda's directness gave no consideration whatsoever to the potential fallout – even when he was the new boy in the class, who had risked financial ruin to become a Formula 1 driver and ended up as an unknown talent at Ferrari for 1974.

'I suppose, as a pragmatic Austrian, that the whole sense of drama was difficult for me to understand. But I like to think that I was pragmatic enough to play the game the way they wanted me to. For example, when I first drove the B3 at Fiorano I told Piero Lardi [Ferrari], who was translating for his father Mr Ferrari, that the car was shit. Piero nervously told me that I really should pull my punches. So I said that it had too much understeer, which it did. So Mr Ferrari told me that I had a week in which to lap one second faster around Fiorano, otherwise I was out.'

Fortunately for Lauda, Mauro Forghieri was already in the process of revamping the front end of the car to give a deeper roll centre and dial out much of the understeer. He easily beat the target that was set for him by Enzo Ferrari and from then on the team truly gelled.

The partnership between Lauda and Forghieri was one of mutual trust punctuated with wild exasperation, as Lauda explained when comparing his era of dominance at Ferrari with that of Michael Schumacher for *Motor Sport* magazine. 'Forghieri was a genius but you needed to control him,' the Austrian said. 'I remember at Barcelona in practice, I came in and told him I had understeer. He said, "You're taking the wrong lines." I asked where, and he said, "Round the back of the circuit." "How do you know?" "Because I have a friend out there who tells me." "Who's your friend?" "Ah, it's the lady friend of my doctor." I said, "Fix my f***ing understeer." He did and I put it on pole.'

Of all those in the management of the Scuderia, it was Forghieri upon whom rested one responsibility over all others, which was to ensure that the cars were competitive. Given the weight of that particular expectation, there can be little wonder that he was described as 'volatile' as often as he was 'brilliant'.

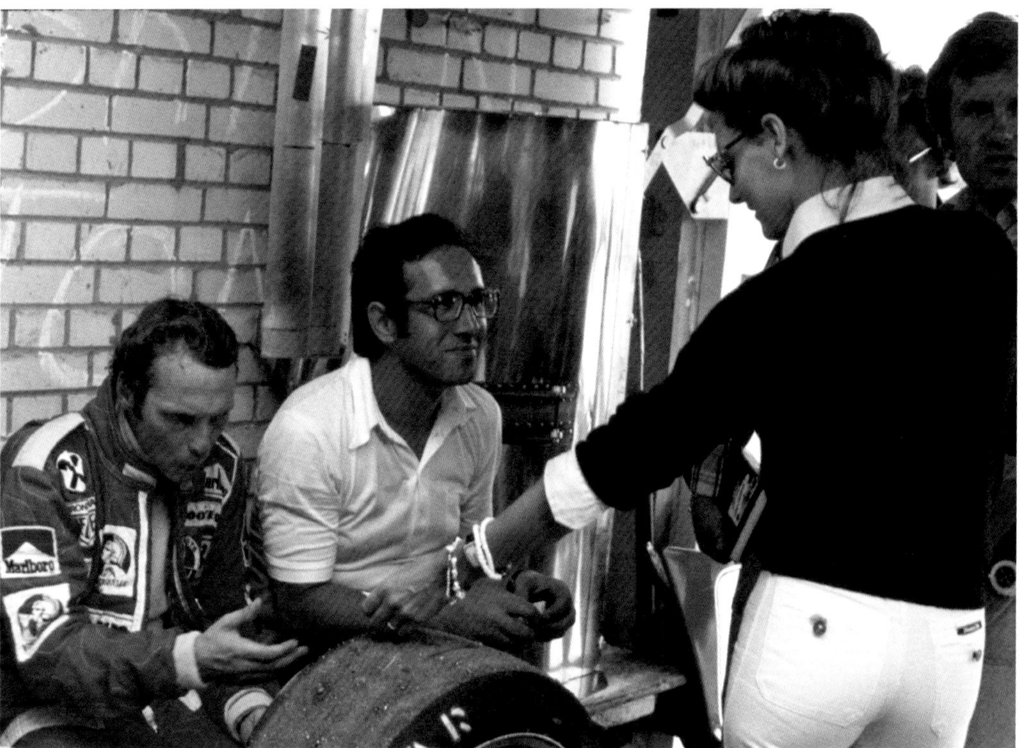

RIGHT The partnership between Lauda and Forghieri moved mountains – and retained a sense of fun. *(Getty)*

MAURO FORGHIERI: THE DESIGNER

Mauro Forghieri was born in Modena on 13 January 1935, the son of Reclus Forghieri, a patternmaker who had worked for Scuderia Ferrari in the 1930s. Mauro was raised in Modena and went to university in Bologna, where he achieved a doctorate in engineering with which he had intended to travel to America and work in the aviation industry.

While to many engineers in the region it may have been an ambition to join Ferrari, Forghieri weighed up the options and realised that salaries were up to 30% lower in Maranello than their equivalents in the USA. Enzo Ferrari offered the young man a job to tide him over until his longed-for American opportunity presented itself. As of 2016, the wait continues...

Forghieri went to work in the engine department under Ferrari's legendary technical chief Carlo Chiti and alongside another young graduate of engineering, Gianpaolo Dallara. It was an engaging role in which Forghieri helped develop the latest iterations of the Dino 156 and 246 V6 engines, the 250 Testarossa and 330 TRI units and numerous other projects across Ferrari's sports car and Grand Prix programmes.

Life was soon turned on its head when Chiti and almost the entire technical and operational team departed the Scuderia in October 1961 to form the new ATS team. Enzo Ferrari, no doubt exasperated, decided to put his faith in young talent and offered the 26-year-old Forghieri the role of Technical Director. So began a period of unprecedented success for the Scuderia in every discipline.

In sports car racing, Forghieri spearheaded the development of Ferrari's new line of mid-engined prototype cars such as the 275P and 330P2, which became insuperable at the Le Mans 24 Hours and Targa Florio, winning World Championships at will. In the GT

ABOVE Mauro Forghieri took responsibility for the cars from concept to reality. *(Sutton)*

BELOW Another of Forghieri's masterpieces was the 330 P4 sports car. *(Getty)*

ABOVE The partnership of Scheckter and Villeneuve was a high point for Forghieri. *(Schlegelmilch/Getty)*

classes, Forghieri also finessed more speed from the 250 GTO and produced its long line of successors. In those days, sports cars had primacy over Formula 1 because they drove road car sales – only after Le Mans had been conquered each year was Forghieri allowed to turn his team's focus towards Grand Prix racing, but even so, developments were fast and positive.

In this new era for the Scuderia's technical department, Chiti's 156 Dino engine was replaced by Forghieri's new 158 V8 unit – and it was this engine that powered John Surtees to the 1964 World Championship in a car that also featured a genuine monocoque chassis. At the end of the year the team debuted a new and exciting powerplant in the gem-like form of the 1512, which used a horizontally opposed V12 design – although Surtees preferred to use the less complicated V8.

The second half of the 1960s saw Ferrari's preoccupation with sports car racing gain strength – spurred on by the arrival of Ford. Detroit muscle was flexed and an extravagant budget was spent in winning Le Mans after Ford's failed buy-out of Ferrari. The GT40 may have ended Ferrari's reign at Le Mans but Forghieri found one of the most satisfying moments of his career when his beautiful 330 P4 coupés crossed the line in a formation 1-2-3 finish at the Daytona 24 Hours, thumbing his nose at Ford on its home soil.

In Formula 1 things were considerably less rosy. After the departure of John Surtees from the Scuderia, the political maelstrom that had ousted him ran riot and had been darkened by the death of Lorenzo Bandini at the 1967 Monaco Grand Prix. A succession of disappointments for drivers such as Chris Amon and Jacky Ickx then followed.

RIGHT After Maranello, Forghieri moved to Lamborghini's V12 F1 programme. *(Sutton)*

The 3-litre era of Formula 1, which began in 1966, saw Forghieri and Franco Rocchi produce the 60° V12 engine – the 312. It was a mighty and sonorous unit but traditional in design and construction, requiring a chassis around it rather than being a fully stressed component like the Ford Cosworth DFV. From 1970 the new horizontally opposed 312B engine put right this omission and delivered the optimum low centre of gravity that Forghieri had been seeking.

Despite these improvements to the team's performance – and its dominance in sports car racing with the 312PB – Forghieri was temporarily ousted in favour of Sandro Colombo from Fiat-owned Innocenti. When Colombo's new monocoque 312B3 chassis delivered Ferrari's worst ever season, Forghieri was brought back and went on to turn the 312B3 into a thoroughly competitive car. He was aided in this during 1974 by Niki Lauda's meticulous feedback from the wheel and by the team of trusted engineers who were present throughout his time at Ferrari.

'It was the same team,' he recalled of the men with whom he turned the 312B3 into a genuine title contender in 1974. 'It was a good one. Engineers and mechanics – Rocchi, Salvarani, Farina, Maioli, Miari, Borsari…'

The success of Forghieri's team in reworking the 312B3 begat the 312T project – his ultimate search for handling agility through combining a low centre of gravity with the minimal polar moment of inertia.

His successes were such that he remained technical chief and de facto team principal through to 1981, when Ferrari hired the British designer Dr Harvey Postlethwaite to bring his chassis expertise and knowledge of carbon fibre construction to bear on the new generation of turbo cars.

At the start of 1985, after winning too little for too long, Forghieri was moved laterally to head up Ferrari's 'advanced research office', leaving Postlethwaite in charge of F1 engineering. It was not a job that he relished, and when Lamborghini decided to go Grand Prix racing he left to become the new team's technical chief after some 26 years at Maranello, rejoining many old faces from the Scuderia – not least former *Direttore Sportivo* Daniele Audetto.

ABOVE Mauro Forghieri remains a vital member of the motorsport engineering community. *(Getty)*

'In fact when I was in charge of the Lamborghini F1 project I asked Mauro to be our Technical Director,' Audetto said, 'and he came with fantastic 12-cylinder engine drawings in his wallet and some of the best engineers from Maranello to work in Modena for Lamborghini.'

The period was ultimately fruitless. Forghieri's 3.5-litre V12 showed promise but was under-funded and suffered from some investors who were less than committed to success. The project folded in 1990.

Soon afterwards Forghieri designed an all-electric minivan, which led to the job of becoming Technical Director at the revived Bugatti marque before he moved on to the Oral Engineering consultancy in Modena. Among the projects he became involved in was the BMW V12 engine that would win the 1999 Le Mans 24 Hours and its first V10 Formula 1 engines.

Today, at 80 years of age, Mauro Forghieri remains active as an engineering consultant working on chosen projects through Oral Engineering. It is more than 50 years since he first made his mark in the sport, but like others of his generation, such as Bernie Ecclestone, the advent of his ninth decade does not necessarily mean resting on his laurels – however many have been accumulated through such an astonishing career.

While the 312T series of cars will be forever to the credit of the technical chief that envisioned them, Mauro Forghieri did not spend every waking hour flitting between the design board, the forge and the lathe. He had around him a team comprised mainly of the same men with whom he had started out at Ferrari, each of whom brought enormous skill and craft to bringing the senior man's visions to life.

Franco Rocchi was the engine expert charged with maintaining the superior power and reliability of the 12-cylinder engines, while Walter Salvarani turned the transverse gearbox from concept to reality, with a team of 50 in the design department and 35 building engines and transmissions.

Another among them was an engineer called Giancarlo Bussi. He was a member of the engine team under Franco Rocchi who, in October 1978, went on holiday to Sardinia and never returned. He was kidnapped by a gun-toting gang who demanded a ransom of two billion lire with the threat of decapitating their hostage. In the end 80 million lire was paid, but everything went very quiet and stayed that way until 2009 when the poor man's skull was discovered in a cave close to where his car had been recovered 31 years earlier. A year later a group of seven middle-aged men was sentenced to anything from 17 years to life imprisonment for their roles in the crime.

At the racetrack, Forghieri generally maintained as much seniority as he did in the factory, but with a different – although no less experienced – team dedicated to the race weekend. These included Antonio Tomaini, the deputy team manager, Ermanno Cuoghi, chief mechanic in the Lauda era, and Pietro Corradini, who continues to work in Maranello tending the Corse Clienti cars.

BELOW The role of *Direttore Sportivo* was to maintain the public face of the team and its logistical needs. *(Schlegelmilch/Getty)*

'I joined Ferrari in 1970 to work in the engine department, where they were building engines for F1, endurance racing and hillclimbs,' Corradini remembered. 'Before Ferrari I had started in 1962 to 1965 with Bizzarrini, then spent four months with Giorgio Neri and Luciano Bonacini developing the Lamborghini 400GT. From there I went to work with Alf Francis on the Serenissima project for four years before joining Ferrari – and to this day I never really left.'

For an engineer of Corradini's experience and calibre, Maranello was a place of the utmost importance – and so too were the men who ran it. 'Ferrari and Forghieri were inspirations for me and I'm very proud to have collaborated with them,' he said. 'Through Ferrari I enjoyed 18 years of the racing department and five years' experience in the production department of road cars like the F40, F355, F456 and F50. We had interesting projects like assessing four-wheel drive – it was a good time for an engineer.'

The travelling party that attended Grands Prix in the 312T era consisted of four mechanics per car, two senior mechanics, two engineers, two truckies and the management team of Mauro Forghieri and the *Direttore Sportivo* – be that Montezemolo, Audetto, Nosetto or Piccinini. Ferrari used two trucks, carrying the two nominated race cars and the T-car, plus sufficient spares to build up two entirely new cars if required. The team also had its own state-of-the-art motorhome and awning for team meals and briefings, staffed by Italian cooks whose handiwork still raises a smile among those who sampled it. Agip sent along its support team and barrels of fuel and lubricants, Michelin operated a vast operation to support Ferrari and Renault from 1978 onwards and Heuer supplied timing equipment for Ferrari's exclusive use.

'In the years 1975–80 the team did not change, the people were always the same group who remained united, changing two to three people maximum,' remembered Pietro Corradini. In equally sharp focus during the years of the 312T were the administrative staff of the Scuderia, led by the Sporting Director – which turned out to be something of a revolving door for much of the 312T era.

It all started with arguably the most charismatic and well-known *Direttore Sportivo* in the team's history: Luca Cordero di Montezemolo. Although a scion of the Agnelli family, his appointment at Ferrari in 1973 was brought about by his passionate defence of Ferrari's performance on a phone-in radio show that Enzo Ferrari happened to enjoy. *L'Ingegnere* sent him a signed copy of his autobiography and followed this with the offer of a job. After moving to the USA to complete his academic career, Montezemolo took him up on the offer.

'My first four years at Ferrari – from 1973 to 1977, when I was the Scuderia's Sporting Director – will always be unforgettable,' he later recalled. 'Those five titles in three seasons were my first professional successes, but it wasn't just that: it was the chance to work with an extraordinary person like Enzo Ferrari and to get to know people with whom I built a relationship based on respect and affection, such as Niki Lauda.

'Ferrari entrusted me with the job of Sporting Director with one sole target: to get back to winning ways. It had been many years since our last success, too many years: the last drivers' title had come in 1964 with John Surtees. We

ABOVE The impressive Ferrari set-up arrives at Watkins Glen in 1977. *(Schlegelmilch/Getty)*

BELOW Montezemolo chairs a team briefing in Sweden, 1975. *(Sutton)*

ABOVE Antonio Tomaini, Mauro Forghieri and Luca di Montezemolo counsel Lauda. *(Sutton)*

needed to put all the parts of the jigsaw into the right places – the team, the working methods, the structure – and to do it in a way that best allowed everyone to carry out their jobs without doubling up: the mechanics had to be mechanics and the engineers had to be engineers.'

Montezemolo threw himself into the task of unpicking the decades-old system of running the team through gossip and innuendo, giving Forghieri's technical team the space it needed to focus on honing its radical 312T into a masterpiece. The pairing of Ferrari stalwart Clay Regazzoni and the ambitious young Niki Lauda was inspired and the two men were afforded much greater input than many of their immediate predecessors – together with a direct route to *l'Ingegnere* if needed. Lauda certainly had no compunction about strolling in to the founder's office or paying a visit to him in the farmhouse at Fiorano if he felt it was required.

BELOW Daniele Audetto achieved dazzling success with Lancia in the World Rally Championship before becoming *Direttore Sportivo* at Ferrari. *(LAT)*

Not that everyone in Maranello looks back on this period in the same way. Some of the old hands in the factory felt that Montezemolo represented Fiat meddling, towards which there was considerable wariness. 'In the early 1970s, Fiat intervened,' said Pietro Corradini, 'first bringing in Colombo as chief designer of a car built in the UK, with Forghieri meanwhile "in exile" in Modena designing the "*Spazzaneve*" F1 car. Then came Montezemolo, who was young and inexperienced.'

As with any period of great change, there was always the possibility for different outcomes to occur at every step along the way – not least the question of which rising young talent it was who would join the team in 1974. Had the Scuderia got its way, it would not have been Niki Lauda lining up alongside Clay Regazzoni, but instead the Austrian's great friend and celebrated rival, James Hunt.

'We needed to turn over a new leaf, starting with the drivers, relying above all on youngsters. Then there were two names on the way up: Niki Lauda and James Hunt,' Montezemolo remembered. 'We tried to take the Englishman and I organised a meeting at Maranello between Ferrari and Lord Hesketh, the owner of the team with which he was racing and who considered him a protégé. But it was like putting the devil and holy water together and nothing came of it.

'So I pushed Ferrari to sign that young Austrian, supported by an old friend of Ferrari's, Clay Regazzoni, who had driven for the Scuderia some years earlier. They were together at BRM and both joined us, forming a very well-matched partnership: one Swiss-Italian who loved life and knew how to enjoy himself and the enthusiasm of the fans, one Austrian who was very quick, determined and exceptional at developing the car.

'In 1974 the title escaped us at the last race, on a weekend in America that still has me scratching my head about how it turned out. But in 1975 everything went perfectly and the results came, with a double championship secured at Monza itself in front of our home fans, a true celebration.

'That was the crowning of a dream that had begun two years earlier, built day by day and the fruits of long days of hard work, evenings spent talking to the drivers, engineers and mechanics and some sleepless nights. It was a wonderful emotion to see the joy of the team and the fans and to feel that, behind those successes, there was also the result of my work.'

For Montezemolo it was a case of 'mission: accomplished'. He was promoted up and out of the day-to-day management of the team by a grateful Agnelli family, taking a less hands-on role with Ferrari while looking at the bigger picture of the Fiat group. To replace him, Enzo Ferrari turned to another bright young manager in the form of Daniele Audetto, who was at that time blazing a trail of success through the newly-formed FIA World Rally Championship at the head of Lancia's works team.

In fact, Audetto would have been given the role of *Direttore Sportivo* before his friend and colleague Montezemolo – were it not for the intervention of Lancia.

'Mr Ferrari contacted me first in late 1973 and offered me to take the role of *Direttore Sportivo* at Ferrari,' said Audetto, 'but Mr Gobbato, General Manager of Lancia and former General Manager of Ferrari, didn't give the authorisation.

'My first meeting with Ferrari was at the end of 1973, my mother received a call from a Signor Ferrari, which is a common Italian family name, and she passed the phone to me saying, "Here, a certain Ferrari is looking for you." I immediately recognised his strong voice and he asked me to go ASAP to see him in his office in Maranello.

'I went the next foggy day, starting at 7:00am, in zero visibility. I managed to find Maranello by 10:00am and I had to wait two hours, with Mr Gozzi showing me around. Honestly, I was not so impressed by the department, compared with the Lancia one. It was little different in my eyes. But the "brains" were in another department that I was not allowed to visit. With Enzo Ferrari at the end we had a good meeting. I can say he liked my ingenuity, passion, dedication, commitment and a bit of insouciance, to offer me the job, despite little experience in F1. But Mr Gobbato the first time said "No!"

'Eventually Ferrari appointed Luca Montezemolo in 1974, and I followed some Grands Prix with Luca during 1975, especially after Reutemann broke his leg in the pit lane in Zandvoort. I was also involved in some meetings at FOCA, that Mr Ecclestone just created to become the start of modern F1, more commercial and with more money involved.'

ABOVE Audetto and Lauda in conference in Canada, 1976. *(Sutton)*

Becoming a familiar face in the F1 paddock while spending his time maintaining Lancia's phenomenal rally success worked well for Audetto. Then the *Direttore Sportivo*'s chair became vacant once again and this time Ferrari got his man. 'After two more years, Gobbato and Umberto Agnelli allowed me to move to Ferrari for all 1976, but "on loan", and Luca was appointed Director of External Relationships at Fiat,' Audetto said. 'But my salary was always paid by Fiat, with the plan for me to return there as soon as the new model 131 Fiat was ready for rallying.'

It would turn out that Audetto's tenure at the *Gestione Sportiva* lasted only one season – but the story of 1976 was one of the most astonishing in the sport's history (see Chapter 6). Not only did the Scuderia's defending World Champion suffer two major accidents in the course of the year but it also marked the first of many bitter clashes between Ferrari and McLaren that have polarised fans ever since.

Emerging from the great storm of 1976, the world looked a very different place in 1977. After a winter of fierce criticism from the press and within Ferrari itself, Niki Lauda was not only coping with the ongoing effects of his injuries but also a deep and wounding mistrust of those around him within the Scuderia.

Agip
speedline
SKF
KONI

The Scuderia would certainly miss having Clay Regazzoni in its midst, who was often a unifying figure. 'Clay Regazzoni was a friend, a gregarious, cheerful man both in and out of Ferrari,' Pietro Corradini recalled. 'He was fun, and over the years he also made many stories that entertain us today, not just his wins and the points he scored.'

Regazzoni's departure made way for the arrival of Carlos Reutemann, in whom Ferrari placed great faith at a time when it was uncertain if Niki Lauda would ever recapture his title-winning form. Witnessing the Scuderia putting its weight behind the Argentine driver deepened Lauda's disillusion with Maranello.

As anticipated, Daniele Audetto had also gone back to his first love of rallying. 'It was planned to launch the new Fiat 131 in the rally "big time" and with investments for the new model,' Audetto explained. 'And for me and for my bosses at Fiat, I had a very good but demanding experience at Ferrari.'

Into the hot seat of *Direttore Sportivo* for 1977 came the former manager of Ferrari's Fiorano test track, Roberto Nosetto. Although well liked by his peers up and down the pit lane and by the staff in Maranello, Nosetto was very much an old-school Ferrari man. His background came from the years of political intriguing that had blighted so many seasons before Montezemolo's new world order was established – and there were many who felt that the team came perilously close to returning to its bad old days.

Nosetto's tenure in the role lasted but a single season, just like his predecessor. Unlike Daniele Audetto, however, his was not a planned departure. The stars aligned in such a way that on Nosetto's watch the team nearly imploded, as first nothing was done to assuage Lauda's mistrust and then the rivalry between the two drivers was allowed to escalate.

Midway through the season it became clear that the Scuderia was in trouble, and from his office *l'Ingegnere* cast his line, seeking a miracle cure for the malaise. What he hooked was a tiny driver with a mighty reputation whose debut with McLaren had left many in the paddock and the grandstands utterly spellbound: Gilles Villeneuve.

The announcement that the Canadian would be joining the team was the straw that shattered the ongoing feud between Lauda and the team. Even as he grimly hammered out his second World Championship victory, the Austrian was finalising a deal that would see him move to Bernie Ecclestone's Brabham team for 1978. With the title won and Ferrari insisting that Villeneuve be entered in a third car from the Canadian Grand Prix onwards, Lauda walked away and took the Scuderia's chief mechanic, Ermanno Cuoghi, with him.

Not everyone agrees on what happened at the time. Pietro Corradini, who stepped up to fill Cuoghi's shoes as chief race engineer, recalled: 'The atmosphere was suffering in early 1977 because Niki could see that Carlos was the driver who could win the World Championship – although I think that the press felt it more than we did.

'Lauda resigned because Bernie and Parmalat offered more money than Ferrari. It is also true that [Brabham's engine partner] Alfa Romeo needed staff who could help them work better with the English. Ermanno wasn't badly treated at Watkins Glen – but when Ferrari knew that he would be leaving with Niki, they fired him and banned him from entering the Ferrari pits, as you would expect.'

None of this reflected brilliantly upon Nosetto. Despite the warmth that he engendered as

OPPOSITE Ermanno Cuoghi was a stalwart of the Ferrari team who departed for Brabham-Alfa with Lauda, allowing Pietro Corradini to assume leadership in the garage. *(Colin Bach)*

BELOW One of the more difficult partnerships in F1: Lauda and Reutemann. *(LAT)*

ABOVE AND BELOW **With 33 years between them, Jacques Villeneuve sits in his father's 312T4 in both pictures.** *(Getty & Ferrari)*

BELOW **Gilles Villeneuve hangs it out in typical style driving 312T4/041.** *(Ferrari)*

THE VILLENEUVE TOUCH

After two seasons of political maelstrom in which the furious battle between Ferrari and McLaren for the 1976 World Championship resulted in the breakdown of trust between the Scuderia and its star driver Niki Lauda in 1977, it must have felt as though the clouds were lifting in early 1978.

'The arrival of Gilles at Ferrari was a time for pure speed,' remembered Pietro Corradini, the Scuderia's chief mechanic from 1978 onwards. 'It was a gamble for Mr Ferrari but the bet paid off – and he loved it!'

It was hardly a glorious entrance for the waif-like Canadian, who found the 312T2 almost impossible to fling around fast and sideways in the manner that he preferred to employ. It was a grown-up car that responded to finesse rather than a heavy right foot – but Ferrari was not unduly worried about that. It already had a team leader in the form of Carlos Reutemann, the man who was judged to be a sufficient talent to carry on Lauda's winning ways. Villeneuve's job was to try to develop into a regular points-scorer who could contribute towards the constructors' championship tally before any other ambitions might be met.

The Argentine team leader won races – including the drive of his life at the British Grand Prix – while Villeneuve settled into learning about life at the sport's pinnacle. What he learned about handling the T-series more effectively, and what he brought to its development in terms of feedback could probably be written on a single sheet of paper, but all was forgiven when he was driving the wheels off the car without worrying about much else in life. As Reutemann said to Nigel Roebuck: 'I like Gilles, and I envy him so much, because he really belongs here, in a Formula 1 paddock.'

Reutemann was not the only man who warmed to Villeneuve's presence in the Scuderia. Everyone did. Even the mechanics who had to replace the parts that wore out or got broken at a rate seldom seen before or since. 'Gilles was not a politician, and was loyal to his team-mates Carlos, Jody and Didier,' said Pietro Corradini. 'He just knew how to be fast – and how well we knew that!'

In May 2012, on the 30th anniversary of Gilles' death, his son Jacques – the 1997 World Champion for Williams after a hard-fought and fractious battle with Ferrari – arrived

ABOVE Jacques Villeneuve emulates his father's cornering style at the wheel of 312T4/041. *(Ferrari)*

at Fiorano. He came to join the entire Ferrari community, including as many surviving team members from his father's era as possible, in tribute. The highlight of the event was when Jacques climbed aboard Ferrari 312T4 chassis 041 – the chassis associated with so many of his father's most celebrated performances in the 1979 season.

It was a surprising occasion in many ways – not only because of the ferocity with which the title battle had been fought in 1997, but also because Jacques had spent so long fighting so hard to escape from his father's shadow. It was hard to blame him, either, because in his early days everywhere that Jacques went there followed the hope of some poignant reflection. Gilles seemed to always arrive before him.

When the younger Villeneuve won the Indianapolis 500 in 1995, the very first question he was hit with was whether he had been thinking of his father as he crossed the line. The reply was terse – just as it would continue to be to any question relating to his father. Those questions inevitably still came nonetheless after his first F1 test, after his astounding debut grand prix at Melbourne in 1996, and onwards through the next two tumultuous seasons towards the World Championship crown itself.

At Fiorano in 2012, Jacques Villeneuve answered the questions about his father with pride. The questions were mostly easy underarm lobs that he could swat away with a wry smile, such as what Gilles might have thought about having a son with the World Championship to his name. 'He would have been happy, because it was his dream to see me become a racing driver,' he said.

Gilles Villeneuve's freakish gifts in controlling a racing car and his relentless drive to be the fastest man on the track created the legend. The affection for him in Italy was redoubled by his passion for what he did. Such passion was

BELOW Friends reunited: original members of Scuderia Ferrari join the Villeneuve family at Fiorano, May 2012. *(Ferrari)*

RIGHT **A lasting tribute: Gilles remains the darling of the *Tifosi*.** *(Sutton)*

not simply reserved for racing – if Gilles was interested in anything, he pursued it with vigour, as his team-mate Jody Scheckter recalled:

'One story sums him up – he had air-conditioning and a fire so he put both on. He wanted to do photography, and bought thousands of pounds' worth of equipment he hardly used. Then he wanted tools, because he used to work as a mechanic. He went to Beta and bought a whole garage full of the best stuff, and never used them!'

Another part of the legend was that the family Villeneuve was always in tow – living in the paddock during European races in a specially commissioned motorhome that would send Bernie Ecclestone into a towering rage at this gypsy camp appearing in the midst of his increasingly professional paddock.

'Gilles having the family with him, travelling with them, was a big thing in Italy,' Pietro Corradini observed. 'Even people who didn't like motorsport liked that – even grandmothers.'

For Jacques Villeneuve, the opportunity to visit Maranello in 2012 was very much a homecoming – shared with familiar faces like Pietro Corradini and the other mechanics, as well as his mother and sister, in the closest environment that they had to a home throughout his formative years – not that the younger Villeneuve regretted that.

'It was much better than going to school!' he laughed. 'Most of the memories I have are from the racetrack, sitting down watching the races. So 90% of what I remember of my father is him as a driver, not home very often, always on the go and if he wasn't in a car, then it was a helicopter or a plane. But that seemed normal, he was my father.'

From her unique vantage point within the team, Jacques' mother Joann was one whose abiding memory was of the relationships that were forged between Forghieri and his drivers. For every indulgence that Enzo Ferrari allowed the *Piccolo Canadese*, there was always a stern presence in the pit garage to keep him focused on the job of developing and setting up the cars.

'Oh yes, they screamed at each other a lot, but they got things done and they progressed,' she later remembered. 'Gilles' attitude was that we say what we have to say and then it's finished and then we get on with it. Gilles thought Mauro was an extremely bright man and admired him very much...'

The feeling was entirely mutual – for all the frustrations that Forghieri may have felt, there was no other man who relished showing him just how fast his creations could go. 'He wasn't taking part in the World Championship, he was simply racing in each race and that was it for him,' said Forghieri. 'He would race with a hastily put together chassis because, at the time, there were only 162 of us, including *Commendatore* Ferrari, and we did not have time to build new cars.'

It was that spirit which so intoxicated the Formula 1 world in the late 1970s and has been so mourned for so long. It is why there will always be graffiti offering up 'Gilles Vivo!' and 'Salut, Gilles!' at the Grand Prix venues where he raced. That little bit of magic – the 'Villeneuve touch' – is as much a part of the 312T series story as its championship wins.

BELOW **'I love motor racing. To me it's a sport, not a technical exercise.' – Gilles Villeneuve.** *(Getty)*

LEFT **Reporting for duty: Villeneuve and Scheckter arrive at Fiorano.** *(LAT)*

a man, the feeling was that he had – to use a football analogy – 'lost the dressing room', and this lack of confidence resulted in his departure at the end of the year. He would go back to the administration of a major circuit – the Autodromo Dino Ferrari at Imola, which he would see become the home of a second Grand Prix for Italy – the San Marino GP – as well as a popular year-round venue, before becoming a senior administrator for the world motorcycle championship.

'Well, Roberto was a very competent and nice man, very professional, he had an unlimited admiration for Enzo Ferrari,' said Daniele Audetto. 'We had probably different personalities, but he did a good job.'

The next *Direttore Sportivo* was young, bright and politically astute. Marco Piccinini arrived in 1978 and would lead the team for the next ten years through times of feast and famine – not to mention the bitter dispute between FISA, the sport's governing body, and Bernie Ecclestone's Formula 1 Constructors' Association. It says a lot about the man that he became a good friend to both Bernie Ecclestone and his right-hand man Max Mosley when Ferrari was leading the charge against Ecclestone's new world order.

Sadly for the Scuderia, its status was only 'best of the rest' in 1978. It joined the rest of the sport in languishing behind Lotus and its era-defining 79. The science of ground effect had arrived and brought with it the chimes of doom for Ferrari's redoubtable V12 engine. Nevertheless, there was still one trump card left to play in the form of Michelin tyres. In 1979 it was the tyres as much as any other weapon in Ferrari's arsenal that kept the 312T4 competitive against the ever-more efficient 'wing cars'.

Another weapon in the team's arsenal for 1979 was its new star driver, the vastly experienced Jody Scheckter. He had been signed in mid-1978 when Villeneuve was still struggling to keep the car on the road and/or in one piece but there was no confirmation which of the drivers would be replaced.

Reutemann had taken this to be a threat to his own future and gone freelance, negotiating a seat with Lotus for 1979, replacing Ronnie Peterson. Thus it would be Scheckter and Villeneuve in the line-up for the last hurrah of the 312T.

'I think the biggest thing I always say with Ferrari is you're racing for the country,' Scheckter reflected on his introduction to the team. 'You're racing for the team but the country's behind you and that's the big difference between it and any other team.'

Fortunately for Scheckter, he was never a man to allow that sort of pressure to get the better of him. What came as more of a shock was how much of a fight he had on his hands to contain Villeneuve's natural speed, building as it was with growing maturity. Although he had insisted on number one status in the team, Scheckter found himself stretched at the start of the year.

'You had to win races,' Scheckter said. 'Gilles was very quick, although I think by the time I won the championship we were equal in poles or I was one ahead of him or

ABOVE Low downforce: Gilles talks tactics with a promo girl. *(Sutton)*

something like that … but what I wanted was to win the championship. So what I had to do was do what I had to do under those rules. And I was lucky enough to get it together in the end. The car was very reliable, never broke down once.'

Despite the very real threat that Villeneuve posed to Scheckter's title ambitions, the good humour between the men was infectious. The journalist Peter Windsor spent a day with the pair testing at Maranello and then sharing a ride back from Fiorano to Monaco. His report remains one of the most enjoyable reads in the history of Formula 1 literature, with Windsor gleefully jotting down every nuance as the two stars bicker good-naturedly throughout the day and narrowly avoid disaster on the highway.

'We spent a lot of time together in Monaco,' Scheckter wrote on the 20th anniversary of his title. 'He liked to dance and he liked girls. He was fun, intelligent and he was a mate. But more than anything, there was mutual respect between us.'

Another example of the easy camaraderie came at the British Grand Prix, when an unsuspecting TV crew attempted to interview Scheckter. Sadly their clear lack of feeling for the subject matter denied them conspicuous success with the South African – and was doomed the moment that his team-mate turned up.

Interviewer: Can you sum up for us exactly what it is you like so much about racing?
Jody Scheckter: The money!
Int: The money?
JS: That's what everybody hates to say.
Int: Is there an awful lot of money?
JS: No … not enough.
Int: Is that what you like about it so much, Mr Villeneuve?
Gilles Villeneuve: I love … I love motor racing and, well, money is nice but it's not the only reason, no.
Int: Can you tell us what the others are?
GV: Well, just because I plainly –
JS (interrupting): Sex. You told me it was sex.
GV: Sex … that's the other reason. Sex.
Int: Is there a lot of that about?
GV: What?
JS: Not enough, either!

Such was the light relief that the two men could enjoy away from the apparently endless rounds of testing that took place at Fiorano, the Scuderia's personal test track. The figure-of-eight track and its associated facilities were built in 1972 to afford Ferrari a significant step ahead of its rivals in terms of gathering data and testing new components and ideas. The construction was inspired not only by the relentless pace of progress but also by the fact that Modena circuit, the rough old airfield that had served Ferrari well for more than 20 years, was no longer suited to low-slung modern cars, and the nearby residents were beginning to chafe at the level of noise being created.

Fiorano was built across the road from the factory, on land surrounding the old farmhouse that Enzo Ferrari had made his base of operations. Throughout the 312T series history he was ever-present, more so than he had

been for decades in overseeing the process of developing the racing cars that carried his *Cavallino Rampante*.

'Fiorano was a training ground for all – cars, drivers and team,' remembered Pietro Corradini. 'Forghieri and his staff were a volcano of ideas and the Old Man was right there all the time, getting the news as it happened. Whenever we tried new parts at Fiorano he asked about them. If there were new parts coming he would ask when they would be put on trial. He could see for himself the performance and the reliability of the car.'

Mauro Forghieri had been instrumental in the design, construction and fitting out of Fiorano as a comparatively space age resource by the standards of its time. 'With the improved data-collecting in Fiorano and the use of computers we could see very small differences,' he said. 'We have 28 timing photocellules and a theoretic perfect trajectory – all data was collected via cable for a central computer to automatically process.'

As a measure of how important a resource Fiorano was in the development of the 312T series, Gilles Villeneuve drove approximately 37,000 miles around the circuit between the end of the 1977 season and the start of 1979. Not only could the cars and tyres gain benefit from such mileage but also drivers could be given every opportunity to deliver points for the team.

From the tradition and single-minded human determination of its founder to the state-of-the-art computer systems that were being built right before his eyes, Scuderia Ferrari was a unique operation in the world of 1970s motorsport – as it has remained to this day. Only Enzo Ferrari could have inspired the 160 or so men and women who developed the 312T series and ran the racing operation that supported it. It was to prove a definitive period for the Scuderia and the sport.

ABOVE A 312T4 and the Villeneuve name return to Fiorano – home of all Ferraris since 1972. *(Ferrari)*

Shell
John Player Grand Prix
YEAR GOOD
1

Chapter Five

The tempest of 1976

The bald facts about the 1976 Formula 1 World Championship season are that Ferrari and Niki Lauda should have cruised to a second successive title with minimal fuss – and for the first half of the season they were on course to do so. In terms of the number of points on the board, Lauda's nearest challenger up to the German Grand Prix was Jody Scheckter in the remarkable six-wheel Tyrrell. But it was the gathering storm between the Scuderia and McLaren that captured all the attention in Italy, Britain and elsewhere.

OPPOSITE Storm warning: F1 1976 was in many ways the most astonishing season in World Championship history. *(Schlegelmilch/Getty)*

ABOVE Audetto, Regazzoni and Tomaini confer with Lauda. *(Schlegelmilch/Getty)*

In all likelihood there was nobody who went into the Formula 1 season of 1976 with a sense of the colossal drama that was about to be played out in the months ahead. Certainly not Ferrari's new *Direttore Sportivo*, the immaculately attired Daniele Audetto.

Unlike his friend and predecessor, Luca di Montezemolo, the new man in the hot seat brought with him proven managerial credentials from anchoring the mighty Lancia rally squad, which was then running rampant in the World Rally Championship.

All of this was a world away from Audetto's background in art – something in which he had excelled as a youth. 'My style was very technological, influenced by Antoni Tàpies, who I met in Barcelona when I was 17. It was "*Informale materico*" with use of different materials, from vinavil, sand and gravel, to ink, oil, drippings and various acids.'

BELOW Ferrari's stars had the world at their feet at the start of 1976. *(Sutton)*

Unfortunately for the art world, life was about to take Audetto along a very different path – one that would take him out of the cerebral world of creativity and ultimately into a knockdown drag-out battle for the World Championship.

'I was intoxicated by the materials I used for painting, and needed several blood transfusions, and doctors had forbidden me to paint for six months,' he recalled. 'During this time I went to the top of the Col de Turini to watch the Monte Carlo Rally, and I was fascinated. I started to take part in rallying and forgot art.

'I was driver first, then co-driver with very good drivers in the Lancia works team, with Sandro Munari, Amilcare Ballestrieri and also with Luca Montezemolo. But after a serious accident Fiorio, the Lancia boss, proposed me to take the role of Sporting Director of the Lancia team, and under my guidance we won many World Championship titles, with the Fulvia first, then the Stratos.'

After narrowly missing out on the Ferrari job in 1973, the opportunity for Audetto to take the reins for 1976 was perfectly timed to meet a lull in the rally programme as Fiat switched its world competition programme away from Lancia and started developing a new car for the mother company. Having received permission for the 'loan' to the Scuderia, Audetto went to work in Maranello.

'I reported directly to Mr Ferrari, keeping a direct line with Montezemolo,' he said. 'I had to manage the drivers, the politics – mainly FOCA and FIA – the logistics, the regulations and talk to the press, a very delicate task at Ferrari, with Mr Ferrari in control of everything, from his office...'

In the early stages of the season, Audetto was sailing the ship through tranquil waters. The new season started with Niki Lauda in dominant form, with Clay Regazzoni claiming a mighty lights-to-flag finish in the inaugural US Grand Prix West at Long Beach, California.

'Yes, Clay had a pure, talented instinct for speed, with less brain then Niki,' said Audetto. 'He liked to enjoy life, parties and women, the opposite of Niki, who was the first real professional intelligent driver, who changed for ever the approach of drivers to F1.

'Clay in Long Beach was untouchable, one second faster than Niki. He liked the place, he

had a good party on the evening before the race, when Niki went to bed with a glass of milk at 10:00pm, after a light dinner...'

Long Beach was to be a fitting send-off for the 312T after a glorious innings for the Scuderia. At the next meeting, the Spanish Grand Prix, the 312T2 would make its debut in what would prove to be the first distant thunder of the season-long storm that would rage between Ferrari and McLaren. Indeed, even the decision to outlaw high-mounted airboxes above the drivers' heads, which was the major visual change of the season, was politically motivated.

'In a meeting in Zandvoort in 1975, the other teams were forced to accept some non-rule solutions,' said Mauro Forghieri, recalling how Ferrari had called up what it believed to be irregularities with other teams' designs as the season progressed. 'To accept them, they asked that the tall air scoop be banned – believing it was our point of strength.'

Such were ever the politics of the 'Piranha Club'. If the calm waters of the opening races had registered a 0 for 'glassy' on the Douglas sea scale before Spain, they were dramatically ratcheted up to 5 for 'rough' in the run-up to the first European race of the season, not only by the airbox rule but also when Niki Lauda suffered major chest injuries as a result of crashing a tractor while mowing the lawn of his new home.

'Well, the "tractor" accident, or motocross-tractor or whatever, was a little silly for a wise man like Niki,' Audetto wryly observed. 'Probably he was not so wise as he would like to appear ... we even thought to replace him for the Spanish GP – he had some broken ribs, and things could become worse if they made a hole in a lung. But Niki is Niki, and raced with a couple of Novocain injections. He managed to finish second, and collapsed at the end.

'I had to be on the podium with James, Gunnar Nilsson and the King of Spain to take the trophy. Without the "tractor" accident Niki would have won the race for sure, even against the illegal McLaren.'

And so the war began to heat up. Having started the Spanish Grand Prix weekend in rough seas, the Douglas scale hit 6 for 'very rough' by the time the chequered flag fell, when Audetto lodged Ferrari's protest against James Hunt's victorious McLaren.

'Well, it was nothing new to me as I was used to fighting in rallies with Renault-Alpine, Ford, Porsche etc, but with McLaren it was more like a "dirty trick",' he said of these opening exchanges. 'They were basically on the limit, and also beyond the rules, to try to overcome the superiority of Ferrari. They made the car illegal in Spain, with the rear wing higher than allowed and an oversize rear track, in a slow circuit like Jarama where downforce was the most important thing.'

Ferrari's protest, artfully managed by Audetto, saw McLaren excluded from the results, pending appeal, although the offending aerodynamics and rear track of the cars were modified for the next few races – causing the team to drop away from the ultimate pace.

The Scuderia capitalised on McLaren's weakened threat, seeing off the challenge of

ABOVE Regazzoni took Long Beach by storm in 312T/024. *(Sutton)*

RIGHT **Lauda pressed home his advantage in Belgium and Monaco.** *(Sutton)*

Tyrrell, Lotus and the rest to win in Belgium and Monaco. By the time of the French Grand Prix at Paul Ricard, Hunt and McLaren were firmly back at the sharp end of the field and at the British Grand Prix the Englishman led the way home to a rapturous welcome – although he would only score points for one of the two wins.

Brands Hatch was full to the rafters throughout the 1976 British Grand Prix weekend, with the undulating 'Indy' section of the track around the start/finish straight taking on the air of an amphitheatre during a bout of Christians versus lions as Lauda claimed pole with Hunt lining up alongside him. Hunt got a poor start, allowing Regazzoni through from the second row, and the Swiss driver – bridling at playing a supporting role to Lauda – stuck his nose up the inside of the leader into Paddock Hill bend. Lauda, thinking that it was Hunt, chopped across the second Ferrari's nose

BELOW **Hunt prepares for landing as chaos breaks out at Brands Hatch.** *(Sutton)*

and Regazzoni was pitched into a spin that launched Hunt over the top of him and also took out Jacques Laffite's Ligier.

Reflecting on that first corner from a distance of 40 years, Audetto remembered: 'As you know, in F1 your first enemy to beat is your team-mate, but Clay was a real gentleman and the accident was a pure, genuine racing accident, in a circuit that was already not ideal for F1, with its start over a crest in a right bend downhill without visibility…'

Although Regazzoni and Hunt had both continued – the former spewing coolant all round the track and Hunt pulling off behind the pits with broken steering – the race was red flagged. What the stewards were not clear on was who would be permitted to take the restart. If they counted the original first lap and only ran the remaining 75 laps, Hunt, Regazzoni and Laffite would be unable to restart, but if everyone restarted over the full 76 laps, it would be an entirely new race.

While they dithered, all three drivers eliminated in the crash quietly rejoined the grid in their spare cars. Then the stewards decided that spare cars could not be used and only the cars that had been on the original grid would be permitted to restart. The three spare cars were wheeled off and, while the McLaren mechanics worked furiously to fix Hunt's broken steering on his original car, the crowd went wild. The booing and jeering from more than 77,000 people caught the gentlemen in blazers by surprise. It unnerved them to think that fists might fly and projectiles could soon be raining down upon them.

Out in the crowds that day was Richard Austin, who would later become a racer himself and end up building the replica Ferrari 312T2s that were used to make the movie *Rush* – which failed to depict this debacle at all.

'Oh God, it was absolutely unbelievable!' he remembered. 'There was stuff being chucked on to the circuit. It was in the days where you could build your own stands and we had a scaffolding tower and we were on the outside just before Paddock, opposite the pit exit. I remember breaking the ring-pull on a can of beer and lobbing it on the circuit. The crowd were going absolutely ape. It was an absolutely unbelievable scene.'

ABOVE Audetto and Lauda study the form at Brands Hatch. *(Sutton)*

The microscopic paddock at Brands Hatch became the eye of a tornado that was ripping through the grandstands – although Daniele Audetto had little time to take in the chaos. 'Brands Hatch was the typical atmosphere of a football match – City against United – with a lot of beer going down. I was concentrating to prepare the protest against McLaren and James Hunt, who did not complete the legal course. He took a short cut just behind the paddock, in front of everybody – and the stewards. He shouldn't have been allowed to restart, and I still don't know how the McLaren boys repaired such a destroyed car in such a short time. I have an *idea*, but no proof...'

Fearing that Brands Hatch was about to be torn apart by a baying mob, the stewards allowed Hunt to take the restart in his repaired car while Laffite and Regazzoni restarted in their spares.

Once again Lauda rocketed off into the lead with Hunt snapping at his heels. Meanwhile, in their wake Guy Edwards' Hesketh was bumped out of the running, Ronnie Peterson's Matra and Patrick Depailler's Tyrrell collided at Druids and Mario Andretti's Lotus was left stranded on the grid. Compared to the abandoned first start this was absolute carnage – but the stewards decided to allow the race to continue at whatever cost.

The furious battle at the front was electrifying, with Hunt and Lauda beating each other's fastest lap time and again. Then Lauda began to slow a fraction – a gear selection problem manifesting itself. On lap 45 Hunt got past

ABOVE On the Brands Hatch podium, nobody wants to look overly certain of the results. *(Sutton)*

BELOW The 1976 German Grand Prix gets under way with Lauda back in the pack behind the McLarens. *(Schlegelmilch/Getty)*

him and, with the crowd now roaring with joy, he stormed through the next 31 laps to win his home grand prix. When asked by the TV reporter what the victory meant to him, Hunt replied: 'Nine points, $20,000 and a lot of happiness!' before stealing a cigarette from an onlooker and heading off on his lap of honour.

Only after Audetto took his protest to the Royal Automobile Club and then the FIA was Lauda duly awarded the victory – when everyone was safely beyond the reach of the British fans and their flying beer cans. It seemed something of a hollow victory to Audetto, however, when Hunt's victory in Spain was subsequently reinstated.

'They were disqualified, but got the points back [from the Spanish Grand Prix exclusion] to "politically" compensate for Brands Hatch,' he said, 'where James, with a broken car, didn't complete the course and yet was allowed the restart, because of the pressure of the public on the stewards.'

With the Douglas scale now tipping 7 for 'high' seas, the field made its way to the Nürburgring a fortnight later and entered the weekend that would define everyone's recollections of that 1976 season. It was a race that many felt should not happen because the safety standards required by the modern sport could no longer be met – and Lauda had been the figurehead of an unsuccessful attempt to boycott the race.

After heavy rain in the morning, all but two cars started on wet tyres but, with most of the track now drying, half the field dived for the pit lane at the end of the first lap – including Lauda. With slicks bolted on he set off with the intention of getting back into the points positions as quickly as possible, but at the right-hand kink before the Bergwerk his Ferrari speared straight on into the earth bank and rebounded, spinning and already on fire, into the path of the oncoming traffic.

Guy Edwards just squeaked past in his Hesketh and immediately stopped. Brett Lunger's Surtees hit the wreck squarely, causing fuel to gush out and burn more savagely, with Lauda – whose helmet had flown off in the initial impact – being trapped in the cockpit as Harald Ertl's Hesketh also clipped the wreck.

For a full minute the Austrian was helpless and wreathed in flame, breathing in searing fuel vapour and smoke until a fourth driver – Arturo Merzario – also stopped at the scene. Between them, these drivers braved the inferno to release their fallen comrade and carry him to safety as the fire crews belatedly arrived.

Although he was initially conscious and talking, Lauda's condition was critical. Even as this drama played out on Italian TV, Lauda's recently departed team boss, Luca di Montezemolo, received a phone call from Maranello. 'Luca? Who are we going to get to replace him?' asked the familiar voice of *l'Ingegnere*.

James Hunt won the race while Lauda was taken by helicopter to Mannheim. He was later transferred to the specialist burns unit at Ludwigshafen where the prognosis led to him being read the last rites. That was the moment when Lauda, enraged by the banality of the process, decided to fight off the Grim Reaper.

Recalling the moment in 2013, he said: 'With a lung problem like I had, you live or you die – and if you don't die, you recover quickly.'

The entire sport was thrown into catharsis – and a temporary truce was called in the war between Ferrari and McLaren, while Audetto marshalled his team and got on with the daunting prospect of relaying between Lauda, the medics and *l'Ingegnere* back in Maranello.

'The big change came after the Niki accident at Nürburgring, and we made too many mistakes,' Audetto said. 'The first was to believe the doctors when they said that Niki was in danger of dying – he even got the last rites from a priest – and Ferrari sent me back to the circuit to ask Emerson Fittipaldi if he would race for Ferrari.'

Fittipaldi, the double World Champion with Lotus in 1972 and McLaren in 1974, was, however, unshakably bound in to his struggling Copersucar team. Indeed, nobody was available to take over the number one Ferrari in the immediate aftermath of the accident.

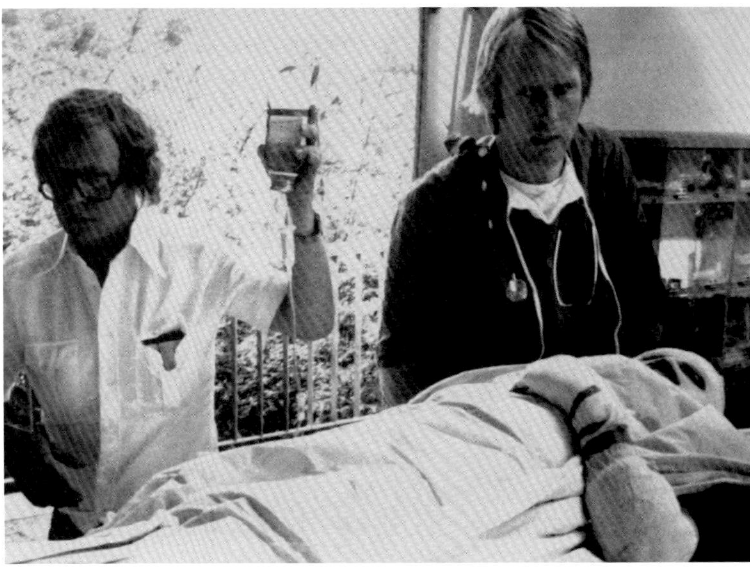

ABOVE The stricken form of Lauda is transferred away from the circuit. *(Getty)*

Meanwhile, Lauda was fighting back from the brink of death, but the doctors were insistent that he would be unlikely to ever race again. Audetto proposed signing Ronnie Peterson, but from his hospital bed Lauda was able to get word to *l'Ingegnere* through Luca di Montezemolo and Luca Agnelli that the Swede's services would not be required.

'Enzo Ferrari was a great man, but you never really knew if what he said was for real or for calculation,' Audetto admitted. 'Sometimes he shouted at me so vehemently that I feared he could start an earthquake – like when he asked me to cancel the Peterson deal, and I tried to

LEFT Audetto was busy juggling all the *Direttore Sportivo*'s roles amid the turmoil. *(Sutton)*

ABOVE **Ecclestone was prepared to let Reutemann go – at a price.** *(Sutton)*

resist – but the following year he admitted that I was right.'

The Scuderia would be absent from the next race weekend, Lauda's home event at the Österreichring, and its attempt to get the race cancelled out of respect for its injured star drew considerable disdain from the paddock and press. The request was rebuffed, as Audetto put it: 'Bernie said "the show has to go on", and the promoters would have lost too much money to pay Bernie's penalties and refund tickets. In fact we were a little naïve ... but romantic!'

While all this was going on, Carlos Reutemann had been successfully recruited to fill Lauda's empty seat. The only problem was

RIGHT **The man who fell to earth – Lauda returns to the F1 paddock.** *(Getty)*

that Lauda was back on his feet and utterly determined to drive at Monza.

'Mr Ferrari was very clear: "Niki, you want to race, I think you are mad, but it is your life and your choice. Come to Fiorano and show me you are fit and fast, and I'll give you the car",' recalled Daniele Audetto. 'It was one of the most intense moments of my life, to see Niki bleeding, pale, a walking dead man, doing his test in Fiorano to convince not only Ferrari, but all the world, that he will race. Unbelievable ... superman!'

With the 2013 release of the movie *Rush*, depicting that crazy summer of '76, Niki Lauda was called upon to share recollections of his return to the paddock. 'It was the most terrifying weekend,' he said. 'I got so upset. I said "Listen, I am fighting my way here, I am fit, here is the proof from the doctors. I have eyesight and can hear, I can drive, I am fit." And those Italian idiots start all over again. So this really broke my balls.

'I couldn't work with the car, I couldn't get used to whatever, the pressure I had on me ... All this bull***t. Therefore on Friday, when I came here, I was stressed.'

Much like Sir Stirling Moss had done when he attempted to get back into the cockpit after his own near-fatal accident at Goodwood in 1962, Lauda discovered that his reflexes and even some basic skills had evaporated – such as finding second gear.

'I could not drive,' he said. 'But in Fiorano three days before I could. I said, "What the hell went wrong?" I had to go back to the hotel, I left the circuit and the whole night I was thinking, "What did I do wrong?"

'Then I made a simple decision. I came here on Saturday; it was qualifying, and I said, "I just drive. I don't want to know any other people's times." There was Reutemann and Regazzoni in the team but I just kept on driving. I didn't care. I got going ... and I was the quickest Ferrari.'

Unlike Stirling Moss 13 years earlier, Lauda decided to race again even without the same instinctive skills that he had enjoyed before his crash. He was still fast enough and he could find no logical argument to suggest that in time the old confidence would not come back. But his presence ensured that the Scuderia was far from being a happy ship, with Regazzoni now contemplating life after Maranello, and Reutemann being held back in reserve potentially untll the start of the 1977 season.

In the meanwhile, the Douglas scale in the war between Ferrari and McLaren got another good kick up to 8 for 'very high' when McLaren was adjudged to have been using illegal fuel at the Italian Grand Prix.

'Another mistake was to race three cars at Monza, with McLaren cheating again with a fuel illegally over the limit of octanes, which I think was *always* used; but I could only ask the stewards to verify their fuel at Monza,' said Daniele Audetto. 'The McLaren should have been disqualified and had the points taken away, but again, the show must go on, and Bernie arranged everything.'

Hunt's times from Saturday were struck from the record and he would line up in 25th place as a result. Recalling the incident many years later, the Englishman was still livid.

'The Monza authorities cheated, as simple as that,' he told Nigel Roebuck. 'According to the rules, you were allowed up to 101-octane, plus an error of one octane. They announced my fuel as 101.7 – still legal, by the rulebook – but as it later turned out, it wasn't even 101! We appealed, of course, but the organisers knew it could only be sorted out after the race had been run…'

ABOVE Lauda catches up with Andretti in the Lotus team area at Monza. *(Getty)*

The circus was meanwhile making its way across the Atlantic, and everything then went in James Hunt's favour for the two North American races – which was unsurprising, as Lauda was still in a fairly catastrophic state. Meanwhile, the world's press was enraptured by the story of the 1976 World Championship, and a pressure cooker was being built around the McLaren and Ferrari garages.

Despite the rancour between their teams, James Hunt and Niki Lauda managed to stay on good terms – despite the best efforts of an ever-increasing number of journalists who were now following the circus. Most had little knowledge of paddock politics, and had editors pressing them

BELOW Bravery personified: Lauda conquered all to finish as the highest-placed Ferrari at Monza. *(Sutton)*

ABOVE Lauda, Hunt and Barry Sheene catch up on the goings-on at Fuji. *(Sutton)*

for deadlines, as Hunt would later recount:

'When I got to the circuit [in Canada, after his disqualification from Brands Hatch was confirmed], the press were winding it up, going to Niki and saying, "James said this" then coming to me, and saying, "Niki said that..." For a few hours we hated each other, but on Friday we talked it through, got in our cars and life carried on as usual...'

Everything would come down to the Japanese Grand Prix. The Englishman was in the form of his life but the Austrian still held a three-point advantage as Formula 1 prepared to make a climactic debut in Japan, in the shadow of Mount Fuji.

Hunt had arrived early in the company of Britain's newly-crowned motorcycle World Champion, Barry Sheene, who was present to offer Hunt what he called 'immoral support'. While the hedonistic Englishmen proceeded to cause havoc, Lauda arrived in a mood of grim determination, exhausted by his injuries, by the politics at Maranello and just keen to end the season.

BELOW Forghieri, Lauda and Audetto in conference at Fuji as the world watches. *(Sutton)*

The story of the race is oft told – that the weather on race day was unacceptably bad, with the circuit flooded by rainwater and buried in fog. What is often overlooked – intentionally or not – is the fact that the tempest lashing Mount Fuji sent the political waters of Formula 1 to the top of the Douglas scale: 9 for 'phenomenal'.

As a measure of just how bad the conditions were on race day, the then-Penske driver John Watson said: 'The conditions weren't difficult; they were just about impossible. When you get rain in Japan, it's not rain as we know it; it's more like a monsoon. The entire main straight looked more like the Serpentine than a racetrack. It was just deep puddles, and even in those days our cars were doing 175–180mph by the end of the straight. The pools were quite deep. Much, much deeper than a tyre would have a chance to clear.'

Having suffered so much from failing to bring about a boycott at the Nürburgring earlier in the year, perhaps Lauda felt compelled to try a different approach in order to win over his colleagues in Japan – and in so doing claim the title. Rather than address the crowd, he entered into a series of man-to-man conversations with as many of his colleagues as he could. In the meantime, the team managers had been locked in meetings of their own, chaired by Bernie Ecclestone.

McLaren's Teddy Mayer later recalled: 'The drivers were not all that anxious to race, James particularly so. Every time we went up there he'd say, "No, no. I'm not going to run." I'd say, "You do whatever you want, James," knowing full well that when the moment came he'd climb in the car. He was saying it's too dangerous, really silly, a joke, and what have you, even though he knew that he couldn't win the title if he didn't go out. I just told him to do what he felt was right when the time came, and not to feel under any pressure.'

In the managers' meetings, Bernie Ecclestone was keen to point out two things:

LEFT Ringleaders in the drivers' debate: Peterson led those in favour of racing, Lauda and Hunt wanted no part in it. *(LAT)*

firstly, that if the race didn't go ahead, none of the teams would be getting paid for schlepping all the way to Japan. Secondly, he pointed out that beyond the paddock there was a colossal audience eager to watch the final showdown between James Hunt and Niki Lauda. Back in London, long-time BBC commentator Murray Walker was in the studio and raring to go, because the importance of this occasion was writ large upon the broadcasting future of the sport.

'It was this race which persuaded the BBC to televise the sport,' he confirmed. 'I remember they opened up the studio at four in the morning, which was something they never normally did. Regular TV coverage didn't start until 1978, because it took time to sort out the question of cigarette advertising, but it was the Japanese race which started the ball rolling.'

All of this was at stake if the drivers refused to go out on to the circuit. If the 1976 World Championship was decided in a meeting room within Race Control, Ecclestone knew that the moment to make F1 a global entertainment would be lost forever – never mind the appearance money.

'It was indeed Bernie that convinced the top drivers just to take the start, otherwise he and all the teams were losing the big fee from the promoters,' Daniele Audetto stated. 'So he said, "We still have the TV satellite. You start, and then you stop, everybody will get the money from the TV and promoters, as legally the race has started."'

Out of all the 26 drivers expected on the grid, only three argued in favour of racing: March drivers Ronnie Peterson and Vittorio Brambilla together with, intriguingly, Ferrari's own Clay Regazzoni. Opposing them were the leaders of the 'no' campaign: Niki Lauda, Emerson Fittipaldi and James Hunt. 'I would rather give Niki the title than race in these conditions,' Hunt said.

There is no great surprise that Hunt was prepared to surrender the World Championship if it meant that he did not have to drive. He was a bundle of nerves and his wild behaviour – such as relieving himself in the pit lane in full view of a packed grandstand and fornicating madly in the team garage – was emphatically not the display of laddish bravura with which it is now often and very wrongly associated.

Daniele Audetto takes up the story: 'So Niki,

BELOW Hunt was living on his nerves in Fuji – resulting in some wild antics. *(Sutton)*

RIGHT **It's over: Lauda climbs from the car and leaves the title to fate as Audetto, in the black jacket, prepares to take a call from Maranello...** *(LAT)*

James and Fittipaldi went to the grid. It was a typhoon going on, but I didn't know at the time that when James informed Teddy Mayer and Alastair Caldwell that he would just take the start and then stop they threatened to end his career, not pay him any money and sue him for breach of contract. And James was already in the car and could not inform Niki.'

At this stage of the story, all 26 cars are on the grid, rain is still falling, light is fading and there is fog on the track. And then the race starts with Mario Andretti on pole position, James Hunt behind him, Niki Lauda third and John Watson fourth. 'Wattie' describes the opening lap:

'You couldn't see where you were. You were totally disorientated. Anybody in the middle of the grid wouldn't have a bloody clue what was going on. You had to rely totally on instinct, and to an extent on whatever peripheral vision you could pick up. Conditions were as bad as I ever had to race in.'

Ronnie Peterson's engine gave up on the first lap, at the end of which Larry Perkins called it quits and pulled his Brabham into the pit lane. Niki Lauda would have been unaware of this and carried on, although a massive spin on standing water during the second lap ensured that he, too, would come trickling into the pit lane and park up next time around. At this point the official story is that Lauda, so damaged by the Nürburgring, had endured enough. What is so often overlooked is that he expected the rest of the field to come in as well.

'And here comes my biggest mistake ever,' Audetto remembered. 'When Niki stopped with Carlos Pace, Fittipaldi and a few more, I didn't have the guts to kick his helmet, push him down in the car, and shout at him: "Now you go, and you stop only when you see James stop as well." But in a flash of memory I could see Niki cold on the stretcher as we helped put him in the helicopter at the Nürburgring, when I was not sure if I would see him alive again. So my professionalism and cynicism at Fuji gave way to my sentiment and to my heart, and it was an error...'

Ermanno Cuoghi, the Scuderia's chief mechanic, remembered that Lauda then went and stood, entirely businesslike, on the pit wall for a few laps to see who else was going to come in. When it became clear that Fittipaldi was going to be the last man to pull in, he walked away, and at that point the two versions of the story – with or without the agreement between the teams – become aligned.

'What actually happened was that we agreed with Bernie that we would do two laps and then all pull into the pits,' Lauda said, many years later. 'That way we would have started the race and fulfilled obligations. I stopped, and so did Emerson and Carlos Pace and Larry Perkins in Bernie's Brabhams, but once they started racing everyone else either forgot or ignored the agreement...'

In fact, Lauda's gamble to stop very nearly paid off when Hunt was forced to pit for new tyres with ten laps remaining, dropping him to fifth place. This prompted the Englishman to launch a desperate chase to the flag. With two laps remaining he sailed imperiously past the two cars that stood between him and the title – Alan Jones' Surtees and Clay Regazzoni's Ferrari.

Third place was Hunt's – although he was unaware of that fact. The lap counters had been unable to keep track of his progress and when Hunt pulled in to parc fermé at the end of the race he was wild; convinced that the title was lost. In his rage it took him an eternity to notice that the McLaren team boss, Teddy Mayer, was holding up three fingers and yelling 'Third! You finished third!' James Hunt was World Champion by one point.

Back in Maranello, Audetto was already clearing his desk as planned, ready to go back to the rally world, but he continued to enjoy a very good relationship with *l'Ingegnere*, who asked him 'to make the first visit to Gilles Villeneuve in Montréal, and to organise a meeting between his son Piero Ferrari and James Hunt to offer him a drive with Ferrari [in 1978].'

Yes – you read that correctly. James Hunt was offered the Ferrari seat for 1978 that was ultimately filled by Gilles Villeneuve – and would have signed, were it not for a hugely lucrative personal sponsorship from Vauxhall, Britain's arm of General Motors, which precluded him from advertising Fiat products.

The prospect of Hunt, Villeneuve or any other driver joining the team was only brought about by the impending divorce from Niki Lauda that was perhaps inevitable in the fallout from 1976. As the Italian media rounded upon him and the Scuderia appeared to put its weight behind Carlos Reutemann, it was an embittered Lauda who won the 1977 title before stalking away from Maranello – as Luca di Montezemolo elegantly observed: 'Something had broken in the jigsaw and the successes of another great year such as 1977 were not enough to put the pieces back together.'

BELOW 'Third!' Teddy Mayer attempts to get through to a berserk Hunt – who has won the title. *(Sutton)*

Movies about motor racing are rare beasts. Good movies about motor racing are rarer still. The most successful motor racing movies tend to mix footage shot of actual racing with a fictitious story, which was as true of the Keystone comedy *Mabel at the Wheel* in 1914 as it was of Steve McQueen's seminal *Le Mans* of 1971 or the 1990 NASCAR epic *Days of Thunder.*

One of the many things that marks out *Rush* – Hollywood superstar director Ron Howard's 2013 retelling of the 1976 Formula 1 season – is that he was not using a contemporary race meeting to tell his story, but instead recreating a specific year in its entirety. Well, sort of.

The film was written by British screenwriter Peter Morgan, whose canon of true stories began with *The Deal* – the story of how Tony Blair and Gordon Brown hatched their plot to create New Labour and carve up the British parliamentary system between them.

This was followed by *The Last King of Scotland* about Ugandan dictator Idi Amin, and *The Queen*, recounting how Tony Blair drove a coach and horses through the British constitution in order to spin Princess Diana's death.

Add in films like *Frost/Nixon,* a tale of the legendary unmasking of the former US president's faulty moral compass in a series of TV interviews, and *The Damned United,* about the rise and fall of Brian Clough, arguably Britain's greatest football manager, and you get the picture. Morgan makes modern history digestible, and many people would accept his version of almost any subject in recent British or Anglo-American history. And it was Morgan who got the ball rolling with telling another factual story his way:

'I live in Vienna and I know Niki Lauda, he's a friend of my wife's, and so I'd spent some time with him and I was always quite interested in him as a character,' he said. 'And James Hunt … I always knew that he was a flamboyant ladies' man and Niki, now that I'd met him, was quite a lot of the opposites. And that, for a dramatist, becomes quite interesting. You've got a real yin and yang cinematically as characters.'

If by any chance readers were to arrive upon the pages of this book after being introduced to the 1976 season by watching *Rush*, then by now they might be somewhat confused. Where, they might wonder, do the references in this book to Hunt and Lauda being old mates come from – surely they hated each other's guts? And why does Watkins Glen only feature once each season, when *Rush* seems to believe that it featured on the calendar at least four times per year?

Let's put it this way: *Rush* is a perfectly decent little film, but it's best to disassociate it from the history of the sport and treat it as a work of complete fiction that looks very much like the 1976 Formula 1 season. Among the many things that look and feel right about the film are the action sequences in which Niki Lauda's Ferrari 312T2 is seen in all its glory – except that for the majority of the film's sequences it is not a Ferrari in action at all.

The movie cars were built by specialist engineering firm Rob Austin Racing, run by British Touring Car Championship regular Rob Austin and his father, long-time racer Richard. They got involved with the production of *Rush* from the outset, when an early shoot required the help of some classic F1 owners.

'It all transpired because I own a 1976 Surtees TS19 that is actually featured in the film,' Richard Austin said. 'We were contacted by the Historic Formula One series about doing a race at the Nürburgring, all expenses paid, to do some trial filming for this forthcoming movie. So we took them up on the offer, went to the Nürburgring and Rob won the race in appalling wet conditions, and then the following day we

BELOW Montezemolo hosts Lauda, Ron Howard, Peter Morgan and the team behind *Rush*. *(Ferrari)*

did some trial filming on the Nordschleife and over that period we got to know Ron Howard and one or two other people quite well. In conversation it became clear that they were going to need to build some replicas and we were asked if it was something we would be interested in.'

The original brief stated that the cars would only need to be cosmetically correct and capable of moving under their own steam at up to 50mph – but this rapidly changed to the point where the cars would be required to reach 100mph and withstand taking off and landing for high-speed sequences set on the old Nürburgring.

'By this time I had highlighted these Formula Novis cars, which were Mygales that were in Portugal,' Richard recalled. 'They had been built for a single-seater series at the Portimão circuit but they were being used for driver training and they wanted to sell five or six of these things. We went over and measured them and the wheelbase was virtually spot on and we did some overlays etc, and thought "yep!" we could make these work.'

A modern single-seater car built for driver training and corporate experiences does not sound like the stuff of dreams – but these humble little cars offered modern safety standards and the right dimensions – all that was left was their appearance.

'We hadn't seen a proper Ferrari 312 but if you remember the Tamiya 1/12 scale models, we got one of those and took it to a place in Coventry where they did a 3D scan of it,' said Richard. 'We blew up the 3D scan and were able to get some templates etc, and we ended up being put on to a guy called Nick Shakespeare of Bespoke Design in Coventry and we got one of the chassis to him and he modelled the shape of the Ferraris out of clay.

'We had it so that the two different top sections of the high and low airbox were interchangeable. We had to contract somebody to make the replica wheels. The centres were slightly different but they looked spot on. Some fabricators in Coventry made the alloy wings and polished them. Everything looked really, really good in the end.'

ABOVE From school car to movie star: Rob Austin Racing built the *Rush* Ferraris. *(Propstore)*

BELOW For the close-ups, the cockpit had to look right even on the replica cars. *(Propstore)*

RIGHT Olivia Wilde played Suzy Hunt in the movie version of 1976. *(Sutton)*

Also involved in making the film were the experts at Hall & Hall, who had a sizeable portion of the 'fleet' of period F1 cars to look after in all weathers. 'We had two McLarens, the 312T, a Tyrrell, a Lotus,' remembered Rob Hall. 'We did 31 days of filming, which was hard work at the time but all our customers were up for it.

'We did a lot of the body moulds for the film because *Rush* just happened to pick on a year where, three races in, they completely changed the look of the cars due to moving the airboxes. We had to make sure that they could start off with the high airboxes and then move to the lower type, because out of all the years in F1 history of course the story they wanted to tell fell in that year.

'We made bodywork for Shadows and McLarens and Ferraris. Obviously we had the 312T that you have photographed here to work with and we made bodywork that was correct for the T2 by chopping the airbox off and putting the gills on the side of the nose. The outline was all the same on those.'

One of the most impressive achievements of the film was the way in which it managed to convert a stretch of Blackbushe airport in Hampshire to look like several of the circuits as they appeared in 1976 – the start/finish line of Fuji, the Nürburgring, Interlagos, Monza and elsewhere was all conjured up using a modular set that could alter the pit lane and grandstands to order and allow CGI to fill in the rest.

When it came to period props, however, no CGI was required – and once again, Hall & Hall was able to help assemble the required hardware.

'The Tyrrell transporter belongs to one of our customers and then we had the Marlboro transporter that belongs to another customer and were able to bring that along as well,' Rob Hall said.

'The vans and buses and cars were all found by the film crew. I don't think many of them could run, they were just sprayed up and worked all right for the film. It was a big budget film and they went into a lot of detail and it certainly helped that Ron Howard was a really nice guy as well.

'When we first met him and the production crew we said: "Look, we're not trying to overcomplicate things but having worked on a lot of films in the past all that we ask is that when we start up we get going because these cars don't like being started then held and then switched off while you change the lighting and then go through it all again. The cars can't sit still, when you want us to go we've got to go." And he understood things like that and was really good to work with.'

Throughout the summer of 2012 there was plenty of excitement about the shoot and the film itself. Scenes were shot at Brands Hatch, Snetterton, Cadwell Park, Donington Park and Crystal Palace. For regulars at British circuits it is fun to play spot the circuit but in terms of the movie-going audience it all gels very nicely.

Indeed, the only problem with that is that those responsible for the film were so insistent that it was as close to a documentary as they could make it. The director, Ron Howard, for example, said: 'The story of the 1976 season and the Hunt–Lauda rivalry is one of those narratives that are so remarkable that you could only do it if it was true. Because people wouldn't quite believe it. And it's got that many sort of twists and turns and that much drama into it.'

Therein lies the fundamental flaw with *Rush*: its creators insist that it is a docu-drama about the events of 1976 when in fact it is a fabrication virtually from start to finish, omitting all but the Spanish Grand Prix controversy and Lauda's accident to rewrite history as something altogether different. But it played extremely well at the box office and scored rave reviews, the monthly movie bible *Empire* saying: '*Rush* will make you pine for a more character-filled, glamorous era of sport – the film captures the point where sponsorship and TV are about to go haywire – but more importantly, it has replaced interest in cars careering round a track with fascination in two extraordinary lives.'

Each review seemed to underline the quality job that had been made of the film – and for his spookily accurate portrayal of Niki Lauda, the German star Daniel Brühl was Golden Globe and BAFTA nominated. It was left to *The Guardian* to question how much actual history there was in the script – albeit as a footnote to what was another glowing review, concluding: '*Rush* takes a mechanic's wrench to a few of the facts, but it puts what is left of them together into a strikingly accomplished and watchable film.'

This is definitely the tone taken by those from the motorsport community who took part in the whole venture. '*Rush* was good as a film. It's obviously done for the masses so you can't sit there and say "Oh, they got that bit wrong and that's not right",' said Rob Hall. 'My memory of the summer of 1976 is that it was blisteringly hot, and we had another good summer when they were filming, but there were races that were held in the rain and they brought in these gigantic sprinklers. We got soaked, the cars got soaked and clearing up afterwards was pretty horrendous but that was what they wanted.'

For those who were there at the time it was all taken with tongues firmly in cheeks. Lauda's mechanic in 1976, Ermanno Cuoghi, said: 'The essence of the story is there in the film, if a bit exaggerated. It is too focused on the drivers. For example, it's true that Niki was a great test driver, but he did not design the suspension.'

As for the *Direttore Sportivo* in 1976, Daniele Audetto, whose slender frame and high fashion was turned into a bulky chap wearing an anorak for the film, he said: '*Rush* is a very good movie for the F1 fans of today, more a romance than the real story, but good as a film. Many times the reality is better than films...'

That may be so, but as a film *Rush* performed brilliantly. Not only did the critics love it but on a modest $38 million budget it made $97 million, prompting Hollywood to look afresh for possible stories from the world of motorsport. At the time of writing, a biopic of Enzo Ferrari, the story of the friendship of tragic Ferrari team-mates Mike Hawthorn and Peter Collins and a dramatisation of *Go Like Hell*, the drama of how Ford Motor Company set out to destroy Ferrari at the 1966 Le Mans 24 Hours, are all at an advanced stage.

LEFT Bernie arrives at the premiere of *Rush* – probably wondering where his pivotal role in 1976 went. *(Sutton)*

BELOW James Hunt (Chris Hemsworth) is distracted on the grid, as Niki Lauda (Daniel Bruhl) looks on from his Ferrari during a scene from *Rush*. *(Rex Features)*

Chapter Six

Individual chassis histories

Six different iterations of the 312T series appeared in six competitive seasons of racing, a total of 31 chassis. Almost all of these cars survive to this day – in fact, there are potentially one or two more of them than actually competed with Scuderia Ferrari. The majority reside in private collections and museums, while a select few can still be seen and heard in all their glory at the world's finest historic motor racing events.

OPPOSITE First of the breed: 312T/018 in action, 1975 Monaco GP. *(Sutton)*

ALEXANDRE
DE PARIS
HAUTE COIFFURE
BRITANNIA
PUB
Tiffany's
Club
18
GOODYEAR GOODYEAR
11
GOODYEAR

An average of five new 312T chassis were built by Scuderia Ferrari each season from 1975–80. Remarkably, all of these cars can be accounted for – although confirmation of the full identity of some later cars is not something that is easily achieved, due primarily to the fact that all the focus in Maranello during the 1980 season was squarely held upon developing the new 1.5-litre turbocharged engines. As a result, the T4/T5 chassis programme of 1980 was less of a concern, and with many cars being sold off into private ownership at the time records became a little 'blurry', and required clarification from Ferrari's lawyers in the mid-1990s.

Only two cars were ever completely destroyed in competition – these being 312T2 chassis 028, the car in which Niki Lauda crashed at the 1976 German Grand Prix to sustain his terrible burn injuries; and 312T2 chassis 030, crashed by Gilles Villeneuve at the 1977 Japanese Grand Prix with loss of life to onlookers. One other car, 312T/019, was written off by the factory after a long career as the official test and development car for the 312T series. The rest of the cars still exist and many of them can be seen and enjoyed in public.

BELOW Regazzoni hustles 312T/021 at Kyalami, 1975. *(Sutton)*

312T/018

The first 312T completed made its public debut in Niki Lauda's hands at the South African Grand Prix, where engine problems masked its potential. Regazzoni then used this chassis in Monaco – qualifying sixth and then crashing out of the race. Scuderia Ferrari never used the car again in race trim. In the 1980s renowned collector John Hugenholtz acquired the car from Ferrari and it made its historic debut at the Ferrari Club Italia event at Imola in 1987. A year later it was sold by Christie's at its Monaco auction for $447,889 including buyer's premium and has changed hands twice more since then, becoming a regular favourite at the major historic meetings such as the Monaco Historic Grand Prix and Goodwood Festival of Speed.

312T/019

Built but never used at a race meeting by Scuderia Ferrari. This car was used primarily for component testing at Fiorano and is listed as 'written off'.

312T/020

The chassis number 020 was previously used on a Ferrari 312B3 in 1974. As a result, no 312T was given the 020 chassis number.

312T/021

This was the primary car of Clay Regazzoni's 1975 campaign, used by the Swiss driver in six Grands Prix throughout the year. It made its debut alongside Lauda's chassis 018 at the South African Grand Prix and scored podium finishes with third place in both the Swedish and Dutch Grands Prix. In August, Regazzoni gave the car its only victory in a non-championship event at Dijon-Prenois before it was retired from front-line duty. This is the car that was then handed over to Scuderia Everest for the 1976 season, being entered for two non-championship races in the UK. After being retired from racing duties, 021 was acquired by Luigi Chinetti for use as a promotional vehicle for Ferrari in North America. In 2002 it returned to Europe in the hands of Italian collector Andrea Burani, who has since sold it to a French collector.

RIGHT Lauda in 312T/022 at the ill-starred 1975 Spanish GP. *(Sutton)*

312T/022

Making its debut in Lauda's hands with victory at the non-championship International Trophy race at Silverstone in April 1975, 022 became the Austrian's primary chassis for the rest of the summer, finishing second in the Dutch Grand Prix, winning in France and finishing third in Germany. After Lauda's disappointed sixth-place finish at home in Austria, the car was retired for the remainder of the season, then used by Regazzoni at the 1976 South African Grand Prix. Ferrari sold 022 in 1985 through Duncan Hamilton's dealership in Surrey, to renowned Ferrari collector Jacques Setton, owner of the Pioneer hi-fi company. The car remains in the Setton Collection in Switzerland and regularly attends historic events, although it is currently believed to be up for sale.

312T/023

If there is a definitive early Ferrari 312T-series chassis then this must be it: the car in which Niki Lauda claimed six victories in 1975–76. Its debut was the 1975 Monaco Grand Prix, which Lauda won from pole position. Three more wins followed for 023 in this first title-winning year, in the Belgian, Swedish and US Grands Prix. At the start of 1976 the car was once again Lauda's preferred mount, with which

BELOW Most successful of the breed: Lauda apace in 312T/023. *(Sutton)*

ABOVE Star of our photo shoot – 312T/024 on its way to victory at Monza. *(Sutton)*

he started out with victory in Brazil. A second victory followed in South Africa and 023 ended its front-line career on the podium with second place behind Regazzoni at the inaugural US Grand Prix West in Long Beach. Another of the cars disposed of by Ferrari in the mid-1980s, this was another entry into the collection of Jacques Setton in Switzerland.

312T/024

Seven World Championship races and two wins make chassis 024, the last of the original Ferrari 312Ts built in 1975, no less a part of the type's legend than 023 – this one having been used exclusively by Clay Regazzoni. It made its debut at the 1975 French Grand Prix and Regazzoni drove it in the next four races, ending with his euphoric victory in the Italian Grand Prix that sealed Ferrari's first World Championship titles for more than a decade. Regazzoni retired 024 from the US Grand Prix, but retained the car for the start of the 1976 season, when he took a brilliant victory – his last for the Scuderia – at the new Long Beach street race. As with so many of these cars, 024 then reappeared in the mid-1980s after it had been bought by British computing magnate John Foulston, who raced it in 1985. It was soon on its way into the collectors' market and has changed hands several times, usually residing in Switzerland. Current owner Leopold Hrobsky bought the car in 1996 from the Brooks auction in Monaco for the sum of FF1.665m including premiums, since when 024 has made occasional outings to major historic events such as the Goodwood Festival of Speed.

312T2/025

The first of the T2s, chassis 025 was debuted unsuccessfully by Lauda at Brands Hatch for the 1976 Race of Champions. He then drove it to second place in the contentious Spanish Grand Prix, after which it passed to Regazzoni, who finished second in Belgium and a muted ninth in Germany after Lauda's accident. It would make one more appearance with the Scuderia as the third car entered for Carlos Reutemann at the Italian Grand Prix, finishing close behind the returning Lauda. With its racing history at an end, 025 was then used as a development car, and was tested at Fiorano with a de Dion rear suspension and the infamous 'T6' six-wheel layout. Contrary to the

RIGHT The 312T2 chassis began with 025, seen here in Regazzoni's hands at the 1976 Belgian GP. *(Sutton)*

ABOVE Chassis 312T2/026 became Lauda's principal car for the first half of 1976. *(Sutton)*

urban myths, the car was not destroyed in a fire while in T6 configuration and in the 1980s it was bought by Italian collector Pietro Brigato, who later sold it on to the 'Turning Wheel Collection' of Ferraris owned by Engelbert Steiger and run as a museum and race team from its base in St Gallen in Switzerland.

312T2/026

With two wins in a fortnight at the Belgian and Monaco Grands Prix, 026 got off to the brightest possible start. It was then held back as the spare chassis for much of the summer, including being used by Regazzoni for the restart at Brands Hatch, before Lauda made his astonishing return to the cockpit at Monza in this car. The Austrian then retained 026 for the remaining races of 1976, including the title-deciding Japanese Grand Prix at Fuji, and the first two races of 1977 where he retired in Austria and finished third in Brazil. The car was then mothballed until it was sold to American collector Lou Sellyei, who sold it to Bruce McCaw in 1993 for the sum of $300,000 plus a Mercedes-Benz 300 SL. In McCaw's ownership 026 became a regular at the Monterey Historic weekend at Laguna Seca and various Ferrari exhibitions, until it was bought in 2001 by its present owner, Indianapolis-based Chris MacAllister. Regularly seen in action on both sides of the Atlantic, the car is now one of the biggest stars of the historic Formula 1 racing scene.

312T2/027

This car saw service in the hands of Clay Regazzoni, Carlos Reutemann and Gilles Villeneuve through the 1976–77 seasons. It was Regazzoni's primary car in 1976, making its debut in Monaco and staying with him for three races before the first-corner accident at the British Grand Prix, which required substantial repairs to be made. Out of action until August and the Dutch Grand Prix, 027 then remained with Regazzoni for the remainder of the season. In 1977 it became the spare chassis and was used by Reutemann to finish eighth in South Africa. It was retired from the German Grand Prix onwards but made a comeback at the start of 1978 as Gilles Villeneuve's car for the Argentine and Brazilian Grands Prix. The car was eventually sold to Japanese property magnate and Ferrari collector Yoshiho Matsuda, where it remained on public view in his museum for many years. In 1995 it was bought by German industrial glazing firm owner Peter Fandel before moving to the Ferrari collection of Helmut Gossens in 1997.

BELOW Clay Regazzoni hauls the damaged 312T2/027 round Brands Hatch. *(Sutton)*

ABOVE A short competition career for 312T2/028. *(Sutton)*

312T2/028

This is the most famous and least fortunate of the 312T series – the car that Lauda crashed at the 1976 German Grand Prix. This car made its debut at the British Grand Prix, taking over from 026 as Lauda's preferred chassis. He finished second at Brands Hatch and then crashed with such catastrophic results at the Nürburgring two weeks later, destroying the car.

312T2/029

Built late in the 1976 season, 029 travelled as T-car for the final three races of the year without being used. Thus it started the 1977 season fresh, becoming Carlos Reutemann's primary chassis for the year. Six podiums, including victory in Brazil, were the rewards from a 17-race schedule. It raced 15 times in Reutemann's hands through the year and was T-car twice. Reutemann retained 029 as his choice for the T-car at the start of the 1978 campaign, although it was never used. When Scuderia Ferrari disposed of the car in the mid-'80s it went first to Jacques Setton, who sold it on to Swiss collector Albert Obrist. When the Obrist Collection was sold off, 029 was one of the choicest morsels picked up by Bernie Ecclestone – the man who Reutemann paid off in order to go and race it – and it remains in his private collection to this day.

RIGHT First of the 1977 chassis, 312T2/029 in action, 1977 Brazilian GP. *(Sutton)*

312T2/030

Intended to be Niki Lauda's first-choice chassis for 1977, he won two races in this car – the South African and Dutch Grands Prix. Second places at Long Beach, Monaco and Zolder did much to ensure that Lauda's second World Championship title was secured and then 030 passed to Reutemann after the Italian Grand Prix. Gilles Villeneuve inherited 030 for his Ferrari debut in Canada, finishing 12th, and then came the season-ending Japanese Grand Prix, in which Villeneuve crashed catastrophically. The wreckage was shipped back to Maranello and, on the orders of Franco Gozzi, laid out in component form in the courtyard ready for the Canadian's return to the factory. According to Gozzi, he berated Villeneuve in front of the team for bringing the car back in such a state – and there is certainly evidence that the car was put on display in the courtyard – after which the remains were duly scrapped.

312T2/031

As the last of the T2s, chassis 031 was Niki Lauda's personal mount throughout the hard months of 1977 when he overcame not only his injuries but also the political intrigues and deep-seated rivalries within Maranello to claim his second World Championship title in three seasons. Making its debut with a fifth-place finish at the French Grand Prix, 031 then carried Lauda to two second places in Austria and Britain and victory at the German Grand Prix. Another second place followed at Monza, and then at Watkins Glen a subdued fourth place brought an end to Lauda's time with the car – he left and it travelled, unused, to both Canada and Japan. At the start of 1978 Carlos Reutemann adopted 031 as his own car, finishing seventh in Argentina and claiming a euphoric victory in Brazil before the car was mothballed. When it was sold, in 1979, 031 travelled to San Francisco-based enthusiast Colin Bach, who has retained it to this day in as original condition as possible. Few other 312T-series cars have enjoyed such devoted ownership.

312T3/032

The first of Forghieri's 312T3 chassis for 1978, 032 made its racing debut in South Africa with

ABOVE The ill-fated 312T2/030 in action with Lauda at Kyalami. *(Sutton)*

LEFT Lauda's final title-winning Ferrari was 312T2/031. *(Colin Bach)*

ABOVE **The first of the 312T3s was 032 – here with Reutemann at Long Beach.** *(Sutton)*

Gilles Villeneuve at the helm, where it recorded a DNF. Next time out Carlos Reutemann took victory in 032 at Long Beach. In what was a short racing career, 032 then finished eighth in Reutemann's hands at Monaco before being taken out of front-line service. Another car to have been in the collection of Pioneer hi-fi magnate Jacques Setton in the 1980s, 032 was sold in 2001 to Spanish collector Joaquín Folch, who spent several years restoring it to full running order and has participated with it in events such as Monaco and Goodwood.

312T3/033

The second T3 built became Carlos Reutemann's primary chassis for the 1978 season, in which he drove five times. He crashed out on oil from team-mate Villeneuve's sister car on 033's debut in South Africa, then the car was switched to a narrower-track front end in time for the Belgian Grand Prix at Zolder, where Reutemann missed a gear at the start, causing a multi-car pile-up in his wake, but managed to finish on the podium. Another retirement followed in Spain, but then came the British Grand Prix at Brands Hatch and what Reutemann would later describe as the best performance of his career. After struggling in qualifying, Michelin flew over a new design and compound of tyres for the race, which improved matters to a degree; however, at the front of the field Mario Andretti was imperious until experimental updates to the Cosworth DFV in his Lotus let go and promoted Niki Lauda's Brabham to the front with Reutemann closing in fast behind him. Eventually a misunderstanding between Lauda and Bruno Giacomelli's Alfa Romeo gave Reutemann the chance to dive past; then he held out against a supremely determined assault from Lauda to take the chequered flag. Two weeks later in Germany another DNF ended 033's World Championship career. Gilles Villeneuve later

BELOW **Reutemann on his way to glory at Brands Hatch in 312T3/033.** *(Sutton)*

drove it to victory at the non-championship Race of Champions in 1979, with updated ground effect including skirts. In 1981 033 was sold to Fabrizio Violati to take pride of place in his Maranello Rosso museum in San Marino. When Violati died, the collection was eventually sold off, with 033 appearing in the Bonhams auction at Quail Lodge in 2014, where it passed to an unnamed American buyer for $2,310,000 including premium.

312T3/034

Undoubtedly the most famous of the T3s, this is the car that Gilles Villeneuve used for the majority of his first full season in Formula 1. It was a learning year for the young Canadian and his erratic progress towards the front of the field began to reap the rewards through the latter part of the season. He started putting 034 at the sharp end of the action where, in all honesty, the car had litle right to be in comparison with the sublime Lotus 79 'wing car'. Villeneuve's thrilling battle with Mario Andretti at the front of the field of the Italian Grand Prix remains just a footnote to the day that claimed the life of Ronnie Peterson. Yet for Villeneuve it marked the start of a rich run of form, and just two races later he claimed that euphoric first victory at Montréal's inaugural Canadian Grand Prix and his legend took flight – while sealing the importance of 034 into the bargain. Villeneuve would start the 1979 season in 034 and scored a fifth-place finish in Brazil to mark the car's final competitive outing. Scuderia Ferrari sold it into the ownership of an American collector who suffered a rather serious bankruptcy, as a result of which the car was sold to Pink Floyd drummer and regular Le Mans racer Nick Mason to add to his collection of fine automobiles, operated commercially under the Ten Tenths banner. Unfortunately, the boat carrying 034 to the UK sank en route, meaning that 034 spent several days submerged in seawater. After being refurbished, this most celebrated of T3s became a regular attendee at historic racing events, despite a disastrous appearance at the 1994 Goodwood Festival of Speed. Mike Wilds suffered a colossal accident while trying to set the fastest time of the day on Lord March's driveway, barrel-rolling 034 into a heap of bits. and suffering considerable injury into the bargain. Both car and driver were eventually restored, and Ten Tenths continued to operate the car until 2012, when it was pre-sold at $1,595,000 to an unnamed Canadian buyer.

BELOW Villeneuve in full attack mode in 312T3/034. *(Sutton)*

ABOVE **Reutemann and 312T3/035 in Canada.** *(Sutton)*

312T3/035

Chassis 035 was a stalwart of the 1978 season that plugged on into 1979, being driven by all three of the Scuderia's drivers in that time. Gilles Villeneuve was the first man at the wheel, recording two fairly unspectacular finishes in the French and German Grands Prix. Carlos Reutemann then took the helm and scored strongly – netting third place in Italy and Canada and victory at Watkins Glen. The car was then used by Jody Scheckter for his first two races with Ferrari, the opening events of the 1979 season. By that time the T3 was seriously outdated and Scheckter managed to score only one point in the Brazilian Grand Prix. After a period in mothballs, 035 then went into a private Swiss collection, where it remained until 2000. It was sold at a Brooks auction for $510,038 including premiums, then just three months later was sold on again, by Brooks, at its Gstaad auction for 690,000 Swiss francs.

312T3/036

Six race starts and one podium – third place for Carlos Reutemann in the 1978 Italian Grand Prix – are the main stats on 036. The car debuted in Sweden the same year and was used five times by Reutemann, including his disqualification from the Austrian Grand Prix after being adjudged to have received outside assistance after a spin. In January 1979, Villeneuve used 036 to start the Argentine Grand Prix and was classified in 12th place, although his engine let go four laps from the finish – this would be its final outing with the Scuderia. When Ferrari disposed of the car it was sold to Italian industrialist Enrico Comerio and to this day the car remains in the keeping of the Comerio family.

BELOW **Reutemann in 312T3/036 at the 1978 French GP.** *(Sutton)*

312T4/037

The story of the first 312T4 is something of a mystery. There is no doubt that this is the car with which Gilles Villeneuve stole a march in the World Championship by claiming back-to-back victories in the South African and Long Beach Grands Prix. Villeneuve raced the car once more, to seventh place in Spain, and it was then used as the T-car in France, Britain and Italy. A week after winning the World Championship at Monza, Jody Scheckter drove 037 in the non-championship Grand Prix Dino Ferrari at Imola, where he finished third behind Niki Lauda – who scored Alfa Romeo's last Grand Prix win of any description in his Brabham BT48. It was to be the last appearance made by 037 with the Scuderia, and it was widely believed that this chassis was then stripped and rebuilt into T5 specification and given chassis number 042, as was described in the *Autocourse* of 1980, which says that Ferrari had 'dismantled their 1979 312T4s (037), (039) and (041) and built three T5s – (042), (043) and (044) for South America'. However, in 1981, a long-standing Ferrari customer and personal friend of Enzo Ferrari, Dr Carlo Bonomi, asked if he might buy an ex-Villeneuve car for his collection. Enzo Ferrari approved the purchase and Dr Bonomi was presented with a T4, chassis number 037, as the car in which Villeneuve had won two Grands Prix. At a later date, however, Ferrari 312T5 chassis 042 came up for sale – the car that was understood to have been built using the monocoque of 037. In 1996 Dr Bonomi sold his 037 to leading British historic car specialist Adrian Hamilton, who sold it on to Villeneuve fan David Lucas in New Zealand. At one stage during this period of transition, both 312T4 chassis 037 and 312T5 chassis 042 were parked next to one another – prompting the historian Doug Nye to contact Maranello for a clarification on how this could have come about. Ferrari's legal team wrote back, stating that 312T4/037 was exactly that, stating: 'In essence, during the years 1980/81 Ferrari gave instructions to a third party to fully reconstruct the T4/037 (together with the other T4 models) with all original parts which were available, except those which could have in the meantime been destroyed and those which could not be used anymore, but (to the extent feasible) including such elements which could have in the meantime have been built in the Ferrari F1 T5/042.' Nye took this to mean that in fact 037 was a new chassis built by an outside contractor and fitted with as many original parts that had been used by Villeneuve in 1979 as possible – including the engine, serial 035. Ferrari went so far as to provide a *Certificato d'Origine* from its legal department, citing the engine number although, since Nye's research, subsequent vendors have elected to call it an 'entirely genuine Ferrari 312T4 Gilles Villeneuve tribute'. The car was subsequently sold in 2001 to American historic racer Richard Griot, who regularly raced and demonstrated the car until 2014, when it was offered by Bonhams at its Quail Lodge sale, although the hammer price of $1.4 million was too low and the car did not sell. It remains probably the most enigmatic and usable car with significant Villeneuve history from his defining racing season.

ABOVE Villeneuve pressing on at Long Beach in 312T4/037. *(Sutton)*

312T4/038

The second of the T4s, chassis 038 was significant in achieving three second places in its four World Championship races, of which the third and final was Gilles Villeneuve's drive in the 1979 Italian Grand Prix. This was the race in which the Canadian showed his class by sticking right in team-mate Scheckter's wheel-tracks throughout the race, rather than attempting to pass him, thereby ensuring that the South African would claim the World Championship. A week later, Villeneuve drove 038 once again at the non-championship

ABOVE Scheckter laps Long Beach in 312T4/038. *(Sutton)*

Grand Prix Dino Ferrari at Imola, where it had reportedly been fitted with development parts for the 1980 T5s. He qualified on pole but made an uncharacteristically poor start, allowing Niki Lauda through to take a commanding lead in his Brabham-Alfa. Villeneuve chased back into contention and hunted Lauda down, but his attempt to pass at Tosa saw Lauda retain the lead and claim Alfa Romeo's last Grand Prix win, while Villeneuve was forced to pit and replace his damaged nosecone. Thereafter 038 was used as the T-car for the Canadian and US Grands Prix, then went into retirement. In the 1980s, 038 was sold to Engelbert Steiger for inclusion in his Turning Wheel museum in St Gallen, Switzerland, where the car remains to this day.

312T4/039

Four race starts for 039 saw Jody Scheckter claim fourth place in Spain and fifth in Britain, while Gilles Villeneuve recorded seventh in Belgium and a retirement from Monaco when the transmission failed. It was taken as the T-car for Long Beach, Hockenheim and Zandvoort, but was one of the chassis used less in the T4's title-winning season. According to contemporary reporting, 039 was then stripped down and rebuilt as 312T5 chassis 043 but 312T4/039 later went into the collection of Jacques Setton, alongside his other 312T series. Certainly the car's appearance at events such as the Goodwood Festival of Speed is that of a T4 and there is no suggestion that it is a reconstruction in the same way as that built as 312T4/037.

312T4/040

The holy grail of T4s is the car campaigned by Jody Scheckter on his way to winning what would turn out to be Ferrari's last drivers' title for 21 years. That is chassis 040, which was introduced at Zolder for the Belgian Grand Prix, where Scheckter won. Two weeks later in Monaco he won again and then with this car completed the next seven World Championship races, winning the title with his final career

RIGHT Scheckter in the Silverstone pits with 312T4/039. *(Sutton)*

ABOVE Scheckter in 312T4/040 that he has retained to this day. *(Sutton)*

victory at the Italian Grand Prix. Scheckter also drove 040 in the non-championship Grand Prix Dino Ferrari, where he finished third, meaning that in total the 1979 World Champion made ten racing appearances in this car during his title-winning year. Small wonder, therefore, that Scheckter negotiated the purchase of this car at the end of the 1979 season, which he retains in a collection of landmark cars from his career alongside the likes of a McLaren M23 and six-wheel Tyrrell.

312T4/041

Chassis 041 became Gilles Villeneuve's primary car through the second half of the 1979 season. With it he made six starts and scored second-place finishes in France, Austria and Canada. It is also the chassis in which he drove into legend, going wheel-to-wheel with René Arnoux at Dijon, racing back to the pits on three wheels after a puncture at Zandvoort during the Dutch Grand Prix and lapping Watkins Glen fully 11 seconds faster than anyone else in torrential rain. At the end of the 1979 season, 041 was purchased by Villeneuve's personal sponsor, the Giacobazzi winery, which has retained the car and its close links to Maranello to this day. As a result, 041 has regularly appeared in the official Galleria Ferrari museum and was the car driven at Fiorano in 2012 by 1997 World Champion

BELOW Villeneuve and Arnoux enjoy their classic dice at Dijon – 312T4/041 in front. *(Sutton)*

ABOVE **Scheckter at speed in Argentina in 312T5/042.** *(Sutton)*

Jacques Villeneuve to mark the 30th anniversary of his father's death.

312T5/042

Chassis 042 was the first of the T5 cars built. Given the extremely close relationship between the T4 and T5, the tub of T4 chassis 037 was updated with the parts required to put it into 1980 configuration. It was raced at the first three Grands Prix of the 1980 season, with Jody Scheckter recording DNFs in both the Argentine and Brazilian races in January and Gilles Villeneuve recording the car's third straight DNF in South Africa. Thereafter, 042 was used as the T-car at Long Beach and was then retired. At the end of that 1980 season 042 was sold into private hands, being preserved for many years by leading French 'Ferrarista' Jean Sage.

312T5/043

The second of the 312T5 cars was built from the chassis of a 312T4 – declared by *Autocourse* in 1980 as 039 – and made its

RIGHT **Villeneuve pounds 312T5/043 around Buenos Aires.** *(Sutton)*

debut at the Argentine Grand Prix in January 1980, driven by Gilles Villeneuve, where he recorded a DNF. A full seven months elapsed before it was used again, with Villeneuve finishing eighth in Austria. The car then passed to Jody Scheckter's side of the pit garage for the Italian Grand Prix, finishing eighth, and in Canada was the car in which Scheckter failed to qualify – graphically illustrating how far Ferrari had fallen behind its British rivals over the course of a single season. The car was later presented by Enzo Ferrari personally to the Museo dell Automobile Biscaretti in Turin, where it resides to this day wearing the livery of its final appearance on track, in Villeneuve's hands, at Watkins Glen at the end of the 1980 season.

312T5/044

According to *Autocourse* in 1980, 312T5 chassis 044 was built from the tub of Gilles Villeneuve's history-making chassis 041 during the winter of 1979–80. This information is, however, misleading, because 041 was already safely in the ownership of the Giacobazzi winery by the time that the 1980 season started. Given that 044 was built and ready for the first race of the season in January 1980, it may well be that it was an updated T4 – which would mean possibly chassis 038 or 039. The key to the mystery comes from the letter written by Ferrari's legal team to Doug Nye in 1996, which states that 'Ferrari gave instructions to a third party to fully reconstruct the T4/037 (together with the other T4 models) with all original parts which were available…' Which other models? We have to discount 040 and 041 because they both went, complete and unmolested, to new owners during 1981. Thus logic decrees that the three T4s rebuilt to T5 specification should have been 037 (confirmed as rebuilt to become T5/042), 038 and 039. The fact that all of the resulting T4s and T5s exist today would indicate that all three T4s had new chassis built for them during 1980–81 and were then sold off as 'official reconstructions'. As for 044 itself, it attended ten rounds of the 1980 season but only started in three of them, with its best result being Gilles Villeneuve's remarkable fifth place in the Canadian Grand Prix, when he was forced to use the car – the team's spare – following a first-lap accident that put his first-choice car 045 out of action. It was sold in 1982 to Italian collector Pietro Tognoli, who retained the car for 20 years, taking it out infrequently to mark specific Ferrari anniversaries. It was put up for auction by Bonhams at its Ferrari sale in Gstaad in December 2002 with an estimate of 600,000–800,000 Swiss francs but failed to sell.

BELOW Scheckter and 312T5/044 at Watkins Glen. *(LAT)*

312T5/045

While the identity of the earlier T5s is something of a moveable feast, it can be said with confidence that 312T/045 was the first of the 1980 cars built from scratch. It went on to become Gilles Villeneuve's primary car for the year, and he drove it six times – the most dramatic of which being his sixth place in the Belgian GP at Zolder after he had stopped for fresh tyres and fought his way back to score a point. In his hands this was also the only Ferrari to lead a lap in the 1980 season. Scuderia Ferrari then disposed of the car immediately to the United States, where it has spent much of its subsequent history. American owners included Gary Kohs, Stan Makres and Phil Mebus before, in the mid-1990s, 045 was sold to the important Japanese collection of Kentaro Kato. Five years later it would return to the USA, where it was kept in a museum until 2006 when it was put up for auction by Gooding & Company at its Palm Beach sale, going to an unidentified bidder for $660,000 including premiums.

312T5/046

Another new build T5 for 1980, 046 would become Jody Scheckter's primary car in which he raced ten times throughout the season, starting in March at the South African Grand

BELOW **A rare moment in front: Villeneuve and 312T5/045 in Brazil.** *(Sutton)*

ABOVE Scheckter in France with 312T5/046. *(Sutton)*

Prix. His best result was eighth in the Belgian Grand Prix in what was a terrible season for Scuderia Ferrari and the defending champion, who bowed out at the end of the year. The car itself has resided in an American collection for more than 20 years and is a regular competitor in historic Formula 1 events across the country.

312T5/047

The chassis built up as 312T5/047 never entered service with Scuderia Ferrari at a race meeting. Instead, it was used as the test bed for the forthcoming 1.5-litre V6 turbo engine. As Ferrari 126 C/047 the chassis was instrumental in developing the new engine and transmission for the 1981 turbo car, as well as the all-important underfloor aerodynamics that would see Ferrari create its first genuine 'ground effect' challenger. The lessons learned from 047 would then be transferred into 126 C/049 in time for Gilles Villeneuve to use the car in practice for the 1980 Italian Grand Prix. When its work was done as a test vehicle, 047 was rebuilt into definitive 1981 configuration and sold to Frenchman Jacques Setton to join his extensive collection of Ferrari road and racing cars.

312T5/048

The last in the long line of 312T series racing cars, 048 had a brief and relatively inglorious career, driven exclusively by Gilles Villeneuve. In its three race appearances it finished sixth in Germany and seventh in the Dutch Grand Prix before its final appearance, which was the Italian Grand Prix at Imola. This was the race in which Villeneuve had his gigantic accident at Tosa corner after suffering a right rear tyre blowout on the fifth lap. After this accident 048 was never again raced by Scuderia Ferrari, but it was rebuilt and sold to Swiss collector Albert Obrist to join his remarkable collection of Ferraris. When the Obrist collection was sold off in the late 1980s, via Adrian Hamilton, 048 went to Anthony Wang in the USA. Five years later it was auctioned by Brooks but was a no sale, eventually returning to the UK in the ownership of John Fenning, who has maintained 048 for regular competition use for drivers such as Mike Littlewood and Max Samuel-Camps at a variety of historic meetings around the world. It is currently on display at the Donington Collection.

BELOW Villeneuve in the last of the breed: 312T5/048. *(Sutton)*

GOOD YEAR
GOOD YEAR
GOOD YEAR
2
Agip
Clay Regazzoni
312
FERODO
speedline
SKF
arexons
AVON
32
21
2
PDB 535
NDV 210F

Chapter Seven

Ownership and historic racing

Between 1975 and 1980, a total of 31 Ferrari 312T cars were built. While prolific in Formula 1 terms, this makes the Ferrari 250 GTOs seem mass-produced in comparison. Yet it is the older GT car that is perceived to be the rarest, most successful piece of Maranello's past – currently commanding around 12 times the price of a 312T.

OPPOSITE **A Ferrari 312T will stand out among any collection of exotic cars. Here 312T/024 is the centre of attention.** *(Author)*

While the price of gold has been on a rollercoaster and the price of commodities such as oil has plunged through the floor, the value of old cars has rocketed – putting even art and wine in the shade as an investment. In the most rarefied end of the market place, the top ten most expensive cars ever sold at auction did so in the period 2013–16 and achieved nearly $275 million between them. All bar one were Ferraris.

Yet in such a superheated marketplace, even such humble fare as a Ford Escort MkII cannot help but double its value every few years – indeed, only the dear old MGB remains as constant in value relative to its surroundings as an oak tree in a beer garden.

A late-1970s Ferrari Formula 1 car sits somewhere in the bottom third of the price range between a £20,000 ($28,000) Ford Escort and a £27 million ($38 million) Ferrari 250 GTO, with values around the $3 million mark. This is not a reflection on the engineering that went into the cars or the achievements that they accrued – rather the reasons behind buying them.

To many owners, much of the value of a plaything worth millions is in being able to get behind the wheel and enjoy it – and to share that enjoyment. A Ferrari 312T cannot carry its owner to the pub with an extraordinarily beautiful woman in the passenger seat. Assuming that the owner can actually fit into a seat that was designed for a snake-hipped 20-something, it is also quite hard to drive a Formula 1 car at all, let alone with any sort of panache. But, for those who can, the 312T is a performance bargain.

BELOW Pink Floyd star Nick Mason sold 312T3/034 privately. *(Sutton)*

How to buy a Ferrari 312T

There are just two options open to a prospective new owner who is hunting for a Ferrari 312T series car: private sale and public auction.

The former is a simple enough path. It may be that an existing owner lets it be known that they are thinking of divesting themselves of a car and thus the word goes out on the grapevine. In other cases, a direct approach from a prospective buyer may work.

A recent example of selling privately is 312T3 chassis 034, the famous ex-Gilles Villeneuve car that was kept for many years by Nick Mason's Ten Tenths organisation. This car was pre-sold when it appeared in the classified section of Michael Sheehan's brokerage, Ferraris Online, in 2012.

It appeared with a price of $1,595,000, and its new owner adjudged this to have been 'correct'. As a measure of how fast values rise in the current climate, the next T3 to come up for sale was chassis 033 – a Reutemann car without the same level of association to the magical Gilles Villeneuve and which was in need of a serious overhaul. In 2014 Bonhams sold this car at its Quail Lodge auction for $2,310,000.

Auctions represent the time when owners, enthusiasts and media can congregate and the

whole deal is carried out in public view. In the case of a 312T series car this will mean that it is one of the big stars of the sale that everyone will want to see go under the gavel and will expect to see a new record price set at every sale.

A genuine Ferrari 312T series car will only appear in one of the headline sales that are held by the premier league of motoring auctioneers, including RM/Sotheby's, Coys of Kensington, and Bonhams – which has taken on several key staff and events since Christies elected to bow out of the historic car market. Of this triumvirate, it is Bonhams that has cornered the market in selling Ferrari 312T series in recent years.

'Bonhams' motoring department globally is approaching about 20 car sales per year, of which five are in the United States,' said Mark Osborne, Bonhams Vice President and Head of Business Development & Strategic Relationships. 'Then of course we add to that the one-off sales that we have when one man's collection comes up and we might present it on site from his garage in the country where the collections reside. We're also now holding three sales per year at Goodwood and we thoroughly enjoy those.'

The scarcity of Ferrari 312T series cars in the marketplace is underlined by the fact that, even with this many auctions taking place in the key hotspots of historic car racing and collecting, only two examples have come under the gavel in recent years.

'We simply do not see Ferrari 312T series cars on a day-to-day, month-to-month basis,' Osborne added. 'This is what makes them such exciting properties at auction. When you see a T-series Ferrari it's big news and if it were my choice I would love to see a T-series in every bloody sale we have – they're fantastic! But it's a rare occurrence and a very special occurrence.

'Of course, when it does happen the types of bidders who are drawn out is extremely impressive and you see names that are really from the very top of the collecting ladder for want of a better expression – and why not? These are championship-winning cars from a very romantic period in Formula 1 history and linked to some of the greatest names in the history of the sport.'

Whenever the happy day arrives that a 312T is consigned for auction, it must go through

LEFT Driver histories help make the car's provenance. *(Bonhams)*

a very strict vetting process to ensure its provenance – upon which hangs both the final value and the reputations of all those involved in the sale. Unlike many cars that are consigned each year, however, almost every Ferrari 312T has celebrity status among fans and collectors – although it must still go through its assessment.

'When I look at Formula 1 cars for consignment, I want to know first whether it has won a race,' Mark Osborne explained. 'There's a good number of potential buyers out there but one or two will only buy a car if it has been victorious and it has the right pedigree, so what I'm looking for is who the driver was and which race it won; then you go to the history and condition.

'It also helps, when we're consigning F1 cars, if cars happen to sit within the top ten designs of any given period. The 312T series, I would say, belongs in the modern period of Formula 1 cars at auction – from the

BELOW Bonhams sold 312T3/033 – twice a winner at Brands Hatch. *(Bonhams)*

ABOVE Chassis plates decree much of the value of a car. *(Bonhams)*

monocoque Lotus 25 up to around the 1980s – and the T-series very much sits in that top ten for that period. This is a unique series of cars and, almost without exception, every one of them is something that you'd want to see at your auction.

'I think the T2 with the nicer intakes on the side of the nose is a particularly beautiful car and it claimed two championships, so it's a strong argument to say that it's the ultimate of the breed.'

There is also the crucial element of which driver is most closely associated with the specific chassis that is being sold. There are two World Champions to choose from – Niki Lauda and Jody Scheckter – and everyone who drove 312Ts for Scuderia Ferrari scored at least two Grand Prix wins. Then of course there is the ongoing phenomenon that is Gilles Villeneuve: the man who turned driving skill into cult superstardom like no other.

BELOW Restoration is not for the faint-hearted, and decisions on usability versus originality await. *(Bonhams)*

'Personalities play a large part in valuation,' Mark Osborne confirmed. 'For millions of people around the world, Gilles Villeneuve was the anointed golden boy at Ferrari and he has a fanatical following. I've been to various races in Europe and North America where cars that he has driven just draw a crowd few other cars can match.

'From the perspective of a sale, however, Jody Scheckter has got his championship-winning car, and goodness me, if that ever came on to the market – the car that was driven at Monza to win the title and has been retained by Scheckter ever since – well, that would be a very special happening in the auction world if it ever got consigned.'

The most recent of the type that has been seen at auction was the ex-Reutemann 312T3, chassis 033, which claimed the great Argentine's nail-biting victory in the British Grand Prix at Brands Hatch in 1978 and would win again at Brands Hatch in Gilles Villeneuve's hands in another thriller at the non-championship Race of Champions.

This appearance effectively marked the end of 033's front-line career. It was then sold on 18 March 1981, eventually to join Fabrizio Violati's *Collezione Maranello Rosso* in San Marino. Oddly, the car's appearance was somewhat amateurishly updated over the years, including the racing number 27 and turning the rear wing endplates red instead of natural metal finish.

The last time that 033 turned a wheel was in 1987 at the 40th anniversary of Ferrari as a constructor, held at Imola. Some 27 years later the car was offered by Bonhams absolutely as seen, requiring expert assessment, investigation and recommissioning work to fully assess the level of work required to return it to peak condition, never mind the possibility of seeing it return to running order.

Despite the significant amount of work that would be required on the car even to put it back on public display, the sale was a rip-roaring success. 'We estimated it from about $1.5 million and its final price was closer to $2.5 million and there was very spirited bidding on it,' Mark Osborne said.

The bidding may have been spirited but its buyer remained silent in the aftermath. Their identity remains a mystery and from that day to this chassis 033 has disappeared from view – one of several Ferrari 312Ts that are cloistered away. For many years this was the rule rather than the exception, but thanks to the ever-increasing array of classic motorsport events that fills the summer months each year, it is now quite probable that avid fans will see and hear a 312T in action somewhere along the way.

'I think the mood now is to use the cars more – perhaps that wasn't the case for a long time, but now, as a collector and a driver, you're presented with these wonderful events to participate in – I'm thinking of the "high airbox F1" demonstration at the Goodwood Members' Meeting, for example,' Mark Osborne said. 'So when I talk to people about buying a 312T series car these days, we're not far into the conversation about a prospective car before they say: "When was it last run and is it going to be ready to use next season?" I think that the mood now is to get into these cars and use them, which wasn't always the case.'

Preparing and maintaining a Ferrari 312T

Having spent the required sum to purchase a Ferrari 312T, the new owner is then confronted by the question of what to do with it. Even if a car is going to stand idle it needs to be maintained: rubber denatures and seals perish, hydraulics leak and wires get brittle. So, if it needs to be kept in peak condition anyway, why not exercise it every once in a while?

Of course, no Formula 1 car is the sort of thing that can be jumped into, fired up and driven off. It is vitally important to ensure that both car and driver are in perfect harmony – or at least broad alignment – before heading out on to the track.

As the man who has sold more 312Ts in recent years than any other auctioneer, and an experienced hand when it comes to driving historic racing cars, Mark Osborne is very clear on what a new owner's first steps should be – even with a car that starts 'on the button'.

'There are a number of people, such as Hall & Hall in the UK or Phil Reilly in the USA, who know exactly what they're doing and can run these cars and get them sorted out for you. I

ABOVE It will take a while to restore 312T3/033 to her former glory. *(Bonhams)*

BELOW The temptation to enjoy driving such a car must be strong. *(Bonhams)*

RIGHT Jody Scheckter hasn't been parted from 312T4/040 for more than 35 years. *(Ferrari)*

would always say that a car should be taken to one of the recognised specialists in the field to make sure that they're happy.'

Being an acknowledged expert on all things to do with the 3.0-litre Formula 1 era of the '70s – amongst many other types of historic racing car to cross his threshold in a given year – Rob Hall of the renowned preparation firm Hall & Hall has plenty of experience to call upon with Ferrari 312Ts. Whether presented with a basket case or a concours winner, his specialist team in Lincolnshire knows that putting the car on the track requires an awful lot of precision engineering to be inspected and, where necessary, replaced.

'Appearances can be deceptive and you'd need to find out when it was last run – which is the problem with Ferraris, that they end up hidden away in collections more often than not,' he explained. 'Even if it's only been a couple of years since it ran, you have to go back to the basics. It's customer-dependent and budget-dependent, depending on whether they want a full race restoration or just a relatively usable collectors' item.'

BELOW Scheckter and 312T4/040 starred in Bahrain's gathering of champions. *(Ferrari)*

In 2010, the Bahrain International Circuit celebrated hosting the opening round of the season by inviting every surviving World Champion to the official celebrations of Formula 1's 60th birthday. All but two drivers were in attendance and, wherever possible, they were reunited with their title-winning machines and given the opportunity to dust off the cobwebs with some gentle lappery.

Among the assembled legends was 1979 World Champion Jody Scheckter and his title-winning 312T4 chassis 040. Unlike many of his peers in the most elite club in motorsport, man and machine were not hard to reunite, as he

ABOVE **Ferrari's *Corse Clienti* operation will operate a turnkey service – at a cost.** *(Ferrari)*

has owned the car since leaving the team at the end of 1980. Despite only driving it once in the previous 30 years, the South African was delighted by how little effort and expense was incurred to get 040 back out on track.

'It's only the second time that it's run anywhere since the end of the 1979 season,' Scheckter confirmed at the time, resplendent in his retro overalls with correct period branding. 'I took it to South Africa a couple of years ago for a charity event and drove it there. Nothing new was on it; even the tyres. So when they asked me to come here, putting it on a track again, we had a look at it and made sure it's okay, but very little needed to be done or changed. Except the tyres!'

Whether the cars are driven or static, tucking them away in a personal collection is by far the most popular option among owners – although there are alternatives. For an increasing number of owners, the option of placing their classic Ferrari racing car back in the hands of the Scuderia to maintain has also become an option, since the founding of Ferrari's *il Reparto Corse Clienti* operation. Such is the dedication that none other than former chief mechanic Pietro Corradini remains at Maranello in order to bring his experience to bear on classic Ferrari racing cars – including several 312T series.

For wealthy and successful men there is nothing quite like the opportunity to savour their Ferrari racing car on track with all technical worries taken care of by the team, and Corradini ensures that their cars remain in peak condition.

Any post-1970 car can be taken into the *Corse Clienti* programme and maintained at the factory. Turnkey events are then held throughout the year at venues such as the Nürburgring, Fuji, Circuit Paul Ricard and Mugello where the owners simply arrive and drive before heading off and letting the team take over the strain of maintenance and logistics. The operating cost of a *Corse Clienti* programme is said to be in the same league as a private jet – albeit with significantly more charisma.

'It is my pleasure today to go to the track to watch over the F1 cars that have since been purchased by collectors,' Corradini said. 'We still see regularly some of the 312T cars that were built, including an original 1975 car and two T3s. A lot of customers want to use the more modern cars – the V12s and V10s from the 1990s and the Schumacher era – because these are much harder to operate without the factory. But we see the older cars, too.'

If you are in the happy position of having just bought a Ferrari 312T series racing car, it is more than likely that you will want to take it to a specialist preparation and restoration firm to get a thorough assessment of its condition. Just like an MOT on a road car, it is as well to know what areas of the car are likely to require maintaining in the near future irrespective of whether it will be used or not. If the intention were to put the car back on the track, whether competitively or for demonstration purposes, then it would be folly to skimp on the fullest possible assessment.

Just what goes into such an assessment, and the most likely jobs that will be required as a result, is explained by Rob Hall, whose company Hall & Hall currently has a 1975 312T and a 1980 312T5 on the roster of cars that it tends.

'If we had a 312T series car brought in now we wouldn't reinvent the wheel. We would replace whatever parts needed replacing, using the same materials. The first thing to do is take it apart, drain any fluids off and have a look inside by running a borescope over it.

'While everything else is under way, you can have the brakes off, take the master cylinders off, reseal all the brake calipers and put new master cylinders on.

'On the engine you'd do a compression check and make sure it's all OK and has no leaks. A liquid check is important because Ferrari is prone to problems where the front cover is all the water pump and waterways and the mounting point for the engine, and it's all cast in magnesium. All of that was pretty delicate when it was new and it was never all that robust because they needed to save as much weight as possible. If you've got water in the oil the front cover may be corroded, and so you go on and work your way through it.

'Replacing parts isn't as much of a problem

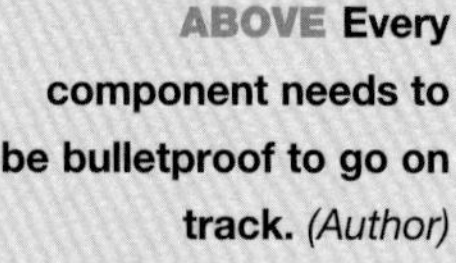

ABOVE Every component needs to be bulletproof to go on track. *(Author)*

RIGHT Fettling one of Forghieri's engines is a considerable job. *(Bonhams)*

as you might think. You know the dimensions of the crank, for example, and what it's made from and you make a replacement. Let's say on the earlier cars they often had rope seals, whereas the later cars had a more effective lip seal, so you would modify it to have a lip seal but that's about all. But we wouldn't be developing the car particularly.

'If the engine's been stood a long time it needs to be stripped, valve springs need checking and so on. Assuming that there are no major problems and everything is about where you want it to be then you put a new filter in, open up the old filter and check it for any worrying signs, and then you would probably put it all back together, wind the oil pressure up, put some fluids in it and reseal the metering unit, and check that the ejectors and blinds aren't brittle.

'If they're stood a long time the oil tank empties and the engine fills with oil and goes straight into the bores. You can never have bores full of oil. So once you check all that and drain it all off you can fire it up. If it has been a while since it started, the engine will smoke like crazy for a while but with a bit of running that should soon clear. The important thing is that it's firing on all 12 – so you check all that.

'Then you check the gearbox. Change the gear oil, use the borescope to make sure the transmission is all right and then it's almost there. You just need to get everything up to temperature then, bleed the brakes, check the shockers don't leak, and from a mechanical point of view you're almost ready to give it a run.

'If the car was just going to do a run at the Festival of Speed or another demonstration event then you'd have the hubs off, crack detect them and that's that. If it was going racing then you take everything off and crack test it: get crack detection certificates on whatever requires it and use common sense.

'For racing, crack testing and certification must be carried out on any structural element of the car. You need to assess the potential results of what might happen if any one of those components were to break. Anything that would have dire consequences gets crack tested. The brake pedal you would test, but not perhaps the clutch pedal. Roll hoops will all be examined.

'Bag tanks would be brand new on a rebuild, and usually we would fit smaller ones than were used in period because we're not covering the same distances and any extra space that results gets filled with foam to give extra protection to the tanks and enhance the safety. After that you can put the car back together and take it to the track knowing that, within reason, you have a reliable car ready to enjoy.'

LEFT Crack testing and ensuring the integrity of components is a vital part of track preparation. *(Bonhams)*

ABOVE **The 312T is more spacious than many F1 classics.** *(Author)*

Fitting the car

Without wishing to cast aspersions upon potential owners of a 312T, it is unlikely that anyone with $2 million to spend on a piece of motoring history will be in their early- to mid-20s or spend several hours per day physically honing themselves to drive it. They will be successful men in their 50s whose natural environment will be the boardroom rather than the running machine, which means that the car was not designed to accommodate them – and although the Formula 1 cars of the 1970s are considerably more flexible in their design than, say, a 15-year-old V10, there are some considerations.

Mark Osborne, the man behind the sale of many historic racing cars at Bonhams, is very clear on the first steps towards the pit lane for a prospective owner: 'At the very least you need to be fitted to the car and get the seat and the pedal box adjusted,' he said. 'I'm a six-footer, and after we closed the viewing I tried to get into the car when we were trying to move it and it took a lot of determination – it was like one of the ugly sisters trying to get the glass slipper on!'

If the car does need a little gentle massaging to accommodate its new owner, then this is another part of the service that is offered by the specialist preparation firms who will assess and upgrade the car ready for going out on track. Getting into a 180mph racing car is one thing, but being comfortable and safe means that the devil is in the detail.

'The Ferrari isn't too tight a fit,' said Rob Hall. 'You take the cockpit cover off that's moulded around the driver, so if they don't fit comfortably in the car you'll make another and make the adjustments – cut bits out or modify the mould. You would make those adjustments on the new piece and leave the original in mint condition hanging on the wall.'

Girth is not the only variable – so too is height. In an age when it is becoming increasingly common for owners to weld roll-over hoops into cars like the Maserati 250F, head protection is increasingly required by insurers and scrutineers to ensure that the old

RIGHT **A little nip and tuck may be required, so keep original parts safely and build new ones.** *(Author)*

cars can continue to be run in our risk-averse and highly litigious age.

'If the drivers are over six feet tall you have to make sure that they're 50mm below the roll hoops, which sometimes means constructing new roll hoops,' Rob Hall explained. 'On a high airbox car you can hide that away, but it can be an issue if you've got a taller roll hoop on a car in terms of how it looks.

'We've had a customer who had an older car with an exposed roll hoop on and he wanted to replace it with a taller hoop in order to compete at Monaco and I said that we could do it, of course, but the chassis number of his car was actually stamped on the hoop! We would have devalued the car significantly, so we had to say that it wasn't really advisable and on balance he decided not to go ahead with the modification.'

However, there are still alternatives that will enable the careful team to shoehorn taller drivers into their cars without demolishing patina, provenance or resale value. 'You can play with things a bit,' Rob Hall said. 'You can bend the floor to fit people's feet in or put a bit of shape in under the dashboard to make space for people's knees. A little bit of work here and a little more there makes a big difference. You want to get it right otherwise the next time you get in the car you're thinking about all the bruises you got last time you drove it.

'We'll usually replace the steering wheel with a quick release – replace the wheel and the column, put the originals in storage and make sure that you've applied the most modern safety standards possible and the original part is safe for the day that the owner wants to sell the car on. But that also gives you a bit more room to get in and out when you want to.'

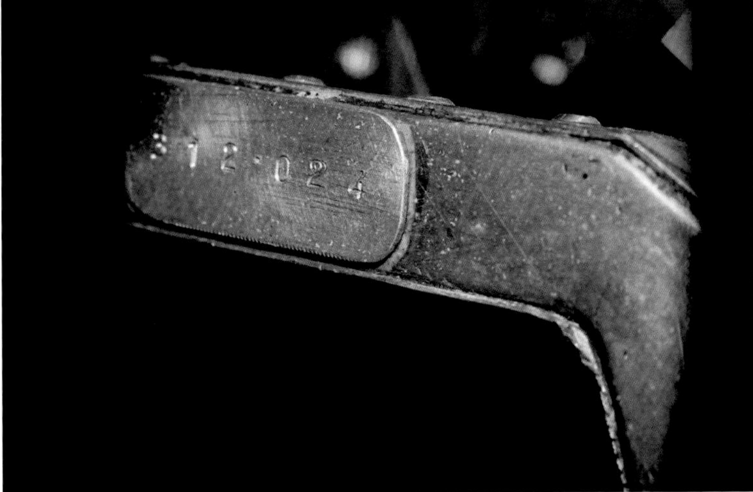

ABOVE Value is driven by originality – like the chassis number. *(Author)*

An owner's view

Identifying the owner of a Ferrari 312T series can be rather hard work. There are any number of reasons why they might wish to remain nameless – which in turn only adds to the air of mystique about the cars. Some may

LEFT Colin Bach made owning 312T2/031 his life's mission. *(Colin Bach collection)*

ABOVE Everything about 312T2/031 is immaculate. *(Colin Bach collection)*

be kept secret in case a spouse (or ex-spouse!) finds out about it. Others for more business-oriented reasons. Others simply because their owners don't have much of a feel for them – they're investments and that's all there is to say on the matter.

Thus it was a delight to encounter Colin Bach, the owner of one of the most important chassis in 312T series history. Not only does Colin have the privilege of keeping his example in some splendour at The Candy Store in Burlingame, California, to be appreciated by like-minded collectors, but he also hosts parties of fellow Candy Store members and other like-minded folk at modern Grands Prix.

BELOW A winner for Lauda in 1977 and Reutemann in 1978, 312T2/031. *(Colin Bach collection)*

In short, if one owner personifies the type of person you would hope owned a Ferrari 312T, it is Colin Bach. His enthusiasm is infectious, enjoying the car is his sole reason for owning it, and after nearly 40 years of ownership this is by no means a speculative investment to be sent off under the auctioneer's gavel when he believes that the market has peaked.

Colin's passion for the Ferrari brand goes back to being ten years of age and watching the premiere of John Frankenheimer's movie *Grand Prix* in 70mm Panavision/Cinerama. The scarlet 1512s driven by 'Jean-Pierre Sarti' and 'Nino Barlini' worked their magic on the youngster – and from that moment on he was hooked on the mystique of Maranello.

It was this same passion that saw Colin broker his first deal on a Ferrari at just 16 years of age. With a fresh driver's licence in his pocket, he convinced his father to lend him sufficient funds to buy no less a car than a 1962 Ferrari 250 GT SWB California – and haggled a fairly remarkable price for it into the bargain.

Although Colin had to sell the car again four months later to repay the loan, his first taste of Ferrari ownership had left him thirsting for more. If it was a wrench to say farewell to the California then it just meant that he would find his perfect car next time around – and this one would be a keeper.

'During 1977, as a mental exercise, I wondered to myself, what would be the ultimate car to own?' Colin remembered. 'A Ferrari, of course. What Ferrari? A Formula 1 Ferrari. Which Formula 1 Ferrari? One which had won the World Championship.'

Having made this decision, it was by remarkable chance that he heard through the Ferrari Owners' Club magazine that a genuine World Championship-winning car was coming up for sale. More remarkable still was that this was not an old ex-Ascari or Surtees car, but a bang-up-to-date 1977 model, driven by Niki Lauda.

'Knowing that there were probably no more than ten or twelve Ferrari F1 cars of any description in private ownership outside the Scuderia itself at that time, I had enormous doubt that this person was in any position to sell this car,' Colin remembered. 'I confirmed this to my satisfaction upon inquiring to him.'

ABOVE **Chassis 312T2/031 in its prime with Lauda at Watkins Glen in 1977.** *(Colin Bach collection)*

The vendor did not actually have the goods to sell – and no wonder. The Ferrari 312T2s were still very much in service, pounding around Fiorano throughout the winter of 1977–78 as the Scuderia sought to gain more knowledge of their new radial tyres and to give its new recruit, Gilles Villeneuve, the benefit of some extra mileage.

Little did the daydreaming faux-vendor know that this particular 21-year-old was such an authority on the marque. Neither was he aware that, having faced such disappointment, Colin would strike out to find a title-winning 312T2 for himself.

'I decided to approach Ferrari directly,' said Colin. 'I had begun a tradition in 1971 of sending a telegram in Italian to *Ing* Enzo Ferrari every year on his birthday (as well as on other special occasions) – for which I always received a written reply from him – and had visited the factory in May 1975. As a result, I was not an unknown outsider.

'Indeed, I had also begun a "pen pal" relationship with his secretary, Brenda Vernor, which has lasted to this day. Nevertheless, I did not approach Ferrari himself. I wrote instead to his financial director, Ermanno Della Casa.

'I had done extensive research and had confirmed that the car which Lauda raced during the latter part of 1977 and in which he won the championship was chassis number 031. I expressed my interest to purchase this particular car. Not long after, I received a pleasant but equivocal response from Della Casa. He very definitely did not say yes, but he also did not say no.'

Even at Ferrari, where movie stars and royalty were welcomed through those hallowed gates, the prospect of a 21-year-old requesting the opportunity to buy a specific Formula 1 chassis must have been unique. To say the least. And he was persistent – writing to Della Casa every three or four months for nearly a year and a half.

'At one point, he offered to sell me a Scuderia Everest F2 car, with a Dino V6 engine, but I told him that I was only interested in the 1977 Ferrari 312T2, chassis number 031. In

BELOW **Avon rubber is de rigueur for historic F1 owners.** *(Colin Bach collection)*

April 1979, for the second consecutive year, I attended the US GP West at Long Beach with the Ferrari Owners' Club. The club always had a large hospitality suite and managed to bring in guests from Maranello.

'Two of them that year were lawyers who provided legal counsel to the factory. I asked them about the prospects of acquiring the car that I was after. They told me – interestingly – that if Ferrari was to sell this car, then it would do so only after the second subsequent model F1 car had proven its competitiveness.

'Gilles Villeneuve won that Sunday – and had also won at the previous GP at Kyalami one month earlier – in the new 312T4. Suddenly things were looking much brighter!'

In late May 1979 a telegram arrived from Ferrari. It was brief but to the point, stating that: 'We are now able to sell you 1977 Ferrari 312T2 chassis 031.' With very few preliminaries, the desired price was indicated – together with the payment details at the Banca Commerciale Italiana di Modena. With that, a very excited Colin busied himself with pulling together a letter of credit, the airfreight arrangements and insurance.

'The car was shipped on Lufthansa from Bologna via Frankfurt to San Francisco in mid-July 1979,' Colin said. 'I cannot tell you how thrilled I was once the car had cleared customs and was in my possession. I was just 23 at that time.'

Without doubt, chassis 031 is the definitive 312T2. It was Lauda's primary car for the 1977 season and, with three wins to its credit, it is the second most successful chassis of the entire 312T series breed.

'To be clear: I wanted this car because, to me, it was the ultimate car. Although there had seemed to be virtually zero chance that I could acquire it, I was determined to do so and I persisted until I did. I considered it the greatest "souvenir" that I could own,' Colin explained.

'It's the seventh and last of the 312T2 chassis and it was driven in nine Grands Prix – seven with Niki Lauda and two with Carlos Reutemann, winning three of those races and finishing in the points all but one time. It is the last Ferrari that Lauda ever raced and it is the car in which Reutemann scored Michelin's first-ever win in Formula 1.'

Having had such a long career, chassis 031 was a car that had raced in the classic Goodyear-shod specification of 1977, and spent a long winter pounding round Fiorano testing Michelin's tyres, new suspension set-ups and new aerodynamics as the basis of the 1978 programme. The 312T2s that were turned out at the start of 1978 were effectively hybrids, halfway towards the forthcoming T3 models.

Having not seen the car before it arrived in California, it was a mystery to Colin exactly what state his prized possession would be in when he first clapped eyes on it. 'The car turned out to be complete and, for all intents and purposes, ready to run,' Colin remembered.

BELOW An unadulterated masterpiece: 031 remains exactly how she left Maranello. *(Colin Bach collection)*

LEFT Maintaining the originality of 312T2/031 means plenty of TLC. *(Colin Bach collection)*

'In fact, as I later learned, Ferrari had sent this car to an outside garage, Sport Auto, where it was returned to its late 1977/ Lauda configuration and livery as well as mechanically prepped. Curiously, all four other remaining examples were "restored" to this same configuration before Ferrari sold them, even though not one of them was raced in the second half of the 1977 season.'

Since then, Colin has maintained the car meticulously but only turned a wheel on occasions, lest he should inadvertently rob the car of some of its prized originality. It might seem to be the ultimate form of self-flagellation, but having worked so hard for so long to secure exactly the car of his dreams, there was never any way that Colin was going to then risk his pride and joy unduly.

'In all my years of ownership, I have never entered my car in a race or even put it in a competitive situation,' he said. 'The closest situation to one that could be called competitive was when Phil Hill drove it in an exhibition "race" in the MHAR at Laguna Seca in 1984. I knew Phil and I was certain that I could trust him implicitly. As I recall, he finished second – behind Bob Bondurant in a 1968 Ferrari 312. For at least two reasons, this may have been the most memorable event in which I have run the car: it was the biggest event in which my car has appeared and I was hugely honoured to have Phil drive it there.

'Also very memorable was the Ferrari Challenge event at Sears Point in 2007, which had the factory support of the *Reparto F1 Clienti*. My car was by far the oldest among the seven cars that were there – the second oldest was a 1994 412 T1B. My car was the only car

BELOW Relishing those rare occasions when the car goes out is part of the ownership experience. *(Colin Bach collection)*

ABOVE Heading the line-up with *Corse Clienti*, 312T2/031. *(Colin Bach collection)*

that did not need any support or assistance from the 16 staff members from Maranello, several of whom I knew. Over the two days of the event, just one or two technicians from Phil Reilly & Company provided all the trackside assistance that my car required.

'By Sunday afternoon and our fourth session on track, only two cars were still running: my car and the 1994 412 T1B!'

Driving opportunities

BELOW Got the car … get the look! Replica Villeneuve lid looks spot on. *(Sutton)*

One thing can be said for owning a Ferrari 312T as opposed to many other Formula 1 cars of the 1970s: it gets you into all the right events. Just like having a supermodel or a pop star for a romantic partner, owning a 312T ensures that invitations are never short, providing one of the most varied potential calendars each year in which to enjoy its performance – and the impact that it has upon aficionados of all ages.

Event promoters want to see crowd-pulling cars on the bill, be that for a demonstration event or at a race meeting. What's more, the enthusiasm for campaigning 1970s 3-litre Formula 1 cars as historic racers was effectively born in the USA – land of showbiz – and they give the crowd a strong return for their ticket-buying dollar.

The Historic Grand Prix association (HGP) was founded in 1974 to provide an outlet for owners of suitable machinery in North America, developing a series of stand-alone 'lifestyle experiences' as opposed to a championship – although these were all competitive occasions. Nevertheless, in the 2010s, support for the HGP dwindled due to factors as varied as the wake of the financial crisis, the increasing value of the cars and increasing resources needed to be competitive, thus the organisation joined forces with the European-based Masters Series.

A calendar of 15 events in 2016 sees seven North American events (including support race slots for the US and Mexican Grands Prix) and eight at classic venues in Europe such as Brands

LEFT A well-known car in historic racing: 312T5/048. *(Sutton)*

BELOW Monaco is a must-attend event. Here American owner Chris MacAllister campaigns 312T2/026 with gusto. *(Sutton)*

Hatch, Spa-Francorchamps and Zandvoort. Key to Masters' ethos is to provide as much track time as possible for drivers, and so most categories will race twice or have a longer pit stop race. With a weekend full of action, Masters competitors can race many different cars across the timetable and then enjoy the excellent hospitality and camaraderie off-track.

The other significant competitive occasion in the calendar is the biennial Grand Prix de Monte Carlo Historique, organised by the Automobile Club de Monaco and held on the Grand Prix circuit in the run-up to the modern event. In 2016 the tenth running of the Historique will welcome cars from 1973–76 – primarily the 'high airbox' types – but as with many events of this nature such as the Le Mans Classic and Goodwood Festival of Speed, the eras selected will change from one running to the next.

Carefully managing the pace of the cars has helped to even out the results in recent years. There was a time where someone with a desire for silverware would buy a fairly pedestrian car – such as a March or Ensign – and spend considerable amounts of money developing it into a much more competitive proposition than it was in period – for a fraction of the cost of buying a Ferrari or Lotus. Today there are checks and balances in place to prevent this and encourage more of the most celebrated cars out, as Rob Hall explained:

'Historic F1 series do want to see the cars out there of course – fans want to see them on the track – so they do try and work out a way to equalise things: V12s are unlimited on revs whereas DFVs are limited to 10,000rpm, for example. That's to try and encourage these cars out.'

Nevertheless, it would be unusual for someone to take all the trouble needed to get their car race-prepared, with all the associated safety upgrades required, if they did not want to be in with a strong chance of going home with a trophy. This means that the owner must choose how much development they wish to fund on the car and, crucially, how many original components will therefore need to be replaced and/or what upgrades they wish to make.

The other alternative to racing the cars is demonstrating them, and the king of all demonstration runs is the Goodwood Festival of Speed hillclimb, which has been held on the grounds of the Duke of Richmond's ancestral home since 1993. With crowd figures now creeping towards 200,000 across four days, including the Moving Motor Show for current motor manufacturers to demonstrate their wares, this is very big business indeed.

BELOW Classic American road courses like Infineon are manna from heaven for a 312T. *(Colin Bach collection)*

Moreover, the themes contained within each edition of the Festival – celebrating a featured marque, some major sponsors and, of course, the overall theme for the event, such as 'Full Throttle: The Endless Pursuit of Power' in 2016 – all help to ensure an enjoyable spectacle for the public and a lucrative corporate opportunity for the organisers.

If the Festival is a target to participate in then the provenance of the car is of paramount importance. A genuine ex-Lauda or ex-Villeneuve car will always stand a better chance of taking part than a Reutemann or Regazzoni car – although if the prospective driver is a big enough draw that might swing things.

If the car is right then its appearance must also be what the crowds want to see – namely the exact finish that it wore when achieving great things in period. This is another part of the preparation service offered by the experts who prepare the cars structurally and mechanically, as Rob Hall explained:

'We would sort out the livery the way the customer wants it – usually the car's best result. We'll restore it to the pictures taken at the event, make and fit the decals and so on and give it the identity that the customer wants it to have.

'Cars evolve through the course of a season, detail changes are made, and you try and accommodate those, of course. It depends on what you want to do. If it's a recommission on a car that's been stood for a while and the owner wants an exact specification that's what we'd do.'

Picking up a bargain

As discussed earlier in the book, the known history of every 312T series chassis exists for all 29 surviving examples – but this does not mean that all are unblemished. Take for example 312T4 chassis 037, with which Gilles Villeneuve claimed two of his three wins in the 1979 World Championship season.

ABOVE A 312T such as our star car, 024, is a real crowd-pleaser at all the best events. *(Mattijs Diemaarts)*

RIGHT Ferrari 312T4/037 has an engaging history. *(Bonhams)*

The actual tub of 037 – the component on which a car's provenance is traditionally fixed – was recycled into 312T5 chassis 042 at the start of the 1980 season. Everything else from the car, however – engine, transmission, suspension and ancillaries – was then all put into a new chassis commissioned by Enzo Ferrari personally.

It was only when a collector held both 312T4/037 and 312T5/042 in his garage that the question was raised of which car was which. In 2014, Bonhams consigned chassis 037 for auction and ended up sending the car back to its owner unsold – although it was an absolute dream in terms of its specification.

'We did offer the T4 that was made for a specific client of Ferrari called Dr Bonomi,' Mark Osborne said. 'It was made out of what they had left of the T4 parts, so that particular car was built by Ferrari from genuine parts and sold to one of Ferrari's customers – which was fine. But what they did was apply a chassis number to it which, in all honesty, they probably shouldn't have done.'

The car was in faultless, race-ready condition and offered with a spare engine for

BELOW All but the tub of 312T4/037 can be traced directly to Villeneuve. *(Bonhams)*

ABOVE Fixtures, fittings and finish were all exemplary on 037 – making it a bargain. *(Bonhams)*

an estimated $1.5–$2 million, which is roughly half what it would have been worth as the original 312T4 with all of its documentation. On this occasion the car failed to sell, but in all likelihood its value will have increased significantly in the interim and, intriguingly, it offers a genuine platform from which to build a potential race winner.

If values for historic racing cars continue to rise at their current rate, it may well be that many will be priced off the racetrack entirely. During the writing of this book the ex-works Ferrari 335 S, as driven on the 1957 Mille Miglia by Peter Collins and Louis Klementaski, was sold for €32.1 million ($36.6 million) – an investment that few would consider risking in competition.

Yet event organisers are effectively in showbiz, meaning that they need to have the box office certainty of the right types of cars – an automotive Jennifer Lawrence or Rolling Stones, which is the category into which a 312T4 would absolutely fall.

The day may yet come when all of the historic cars seen in action are 'toolroom copies' of the most famous cars in the world, rather than actually *being* the most famous cars in the world. Yet given that any racing car that has been in competition for 40 years or more will have had the majority of its parts replaced – an embodiment of the Theseus paradox or the apocryphal 'granddad's axe' that is all original after six replacement heads and eight replacement handles – the question is whether people wish to see these cars in action.

The fact that you are reading this book suggests that the appetite to enjoy cars like the Ferrari 312T remains as strong as ever, meaning that we can all hope to continue seeing and celebrating these cars for some time to come.

Appendix 1

Ferrari 312T series specifications

	312T	312T2
Chassis	Aluminium panels riveted to variable-section light alloy structure and cast light alloy supports	Aluminium panels riveted to variable-section light alloy structure and cast light alloy supports
Body	Moulded composite body and alloy panels, alloy wings	Moulded composite body and alloy panels, alloy wings
Front suspension	Lower wishbones, rocker arms, inboard spring/damper units and anti-roll bar	Lower wishbones, rocker arms, inboard spring/damper units and anti-roll bar
Rear suspension	Upper arm, reversed lower wishbones, top links, trailing arms, coil springs over dampers, anti-roll bar	Upper arm, reversed lower wishbones, top links, trailing arms, coil springs over dampers, anti-roll bar
Brakes	Lockheed callipers and Brembo ventilated cast iron discs all round, rear inboard	Lockheed callipers and Brembo ventilated cast iron discs all round, rear inboard
Wheel size	F: 10 x 13 R: 18 x 13	F: 10 x 13 R: 18 x 13
Tyre size	F: 9.2/20 x 13 R: 16.2/26 x 13	F: 9.2/20 x 13 R: 16.2/26 x 13
Engine type	Ferrari Type 015 180° V12	Ferrari Type 015 180° V12
Engine capacity	2,992cc	2,992cc
Engine construction	Light alloy block and head, aluminium wet liners, 112mm connecting rods, water cooled, dry sump	Light alloy block and head, aluminium wet liners, 112mm connecting rods, water cooled, dry sump
Camshaft	Gear driven	Gear driven
Engine weight	170kg	170kg
Bore and stroke	80mm x 49.6mm 3.14in x 1.95in	80mm x 49.6mm 3.14in x 1.95in
Compression ratio	11.5:1	11.5.1
Maximum power	485bhp @ 12,200rpm	500hp @ 12,200rpm
Maximum torque	236lb/ft @ 9,700rpm	236 lb/ft @ 9,700rpm
bhp per litre	162	167
Power-to-weight	0.84bhp/kg	0.87bhp/kg
Valves	48	48
Fuel system	Lucas fuel injection	Lucas fuel injection
Fuel capacity	200 litres	200 litres
Gearbox	Ferrari Type 015 5-speed manual	Ferrari Type 015 5-speed manual
Transmission	Borg & Beck multi-plate clutch with limited-slip differential	Borg & Beck multi-plate clutch with limited-slip differential
Wheelbase	2.518m	2.56m
Track	F: 1.51m R: 1.53m	F: 1.51m R: 1.42m
Length	4.14m	4.316m
Width	2.03m	1.93m
Height	1.275m	1.02m
Weight	575kg	575kg

	312T3	312T4	312T5
	Aluminium panels riveted to variable-section light alloy structure and cast light alloy supports	Aluminium panels riveted to variable-section light alloy structure and cast light alloy supports	Aluminium panels riveted to variable-section light alloy structure and cast light alloy supports
	Moulded composite body and alloy panels, alloy wings	Moulded composite body and alloy panels, alloy wings	Moulded composite body and alloy panels, alloy wings
	Lower wishbones, rocker arms, inboard spring/damper units and anti-roll bar	Lower wishbones, rocker arms, inboard spring/damper units and anti-roll bar	Lower wishbones, rocker arms, inboard spring/damper units and anti-roll bar
	Upper arm, reversed lower wishbones, top links, trailing arms, coil springs over dampers, anti-roll bar	Upper arm, reversed lower wishbones, top links, trailing arms, coil springs over dampers, anti-roll bar	Upper arm, reversed lower wishbones, top links, trailing arms, coil springs over dampers, anti-roll bar
	Lockheed callipers and Brembo ventilated cast iron discs all round, rear inboard	Lockheed callipers and Brembo ventilated cast iron discs all round, rear inboard	Lockheed callipers and Brembo ventilated cast iron discs all round, rear inboard
	F: 10 x 13 R: 18 x 13	F: 10 x 13 R: 18 x 13	F: 10 x 13 R: 18 x 13
	F: 24/55 x 13 R: 40/65 x 13	F: 23/59 x 13 R: 38/68 x 13	F: 23/59 x 13 R: 38/68 x 13
	Ferrari Type 015 180° V12	Ferrari Type 015 180° V12	Ferrari Type 015 180° V12
	2,992cc	2,992cc	2,992cc
	Light alloy block and head, aluminium wet liners, 112mm connecting rods, water cooled, dry sump	Light alloy block and head, aluminium wet liners, 112mm connecting rods, water cooled, dry sump	Light alloy block and head, aluminium wet liners, 112mm connecting rods, water cooled, dry sump
	Gear driven	Gear driven	Gear driven
	170kg	144kg	144kg
	80mm x 49.6mm 3.14in x 1.95in	80mm x 49.6mm 3.14in x 1.95in	80mm x 49.6mm 3.14in x 1.95in
	11.5:1	11.5:1	11.5:1
	510hp @ 12,500rpm	515hp @ 12,300rpm	515hp @ 12,300rpm
	236lb/ft @ 9,700rpm	244lb/ft @ 9,800rpm	244lb/ft @ 9,800rpm
	170	172	172
	0.87bhp/kg	0.87bhp/kg	0.85bhp/kg
	48	48	48
	Lucas fuel injection	Lucas fuel injection	Lucas fuel injection
	200 litres	200 litres	210 litres
	Ferrari Type 015 5-speed manual	Ferrari Type 022 5-speed manual	Ferrari Type 022 5-speed manual
	Borg & Beck multi-plate clutch with limited-slip differential	Borg & Beck multi-plate clutch with limited-slip differential	Borg & Beck multi-plate clutch with limited-slip differential
	2.56m	2.7m	2.7m
	F: 1.62m R: 1.53m	F: 1.7m R: 1.6m	F: 1.7m R: 1.6m
	4.23m	4.46m	4.53m
	2.13m	2.12m	2.12m
	1.01m	1.01m	1.02m
	580kg	590kg	595kg

Appendix 2

Ferrari 312T series Grand Prix race history

1975					
Date	**Race**	**Circuit**	**No. Driver (Chassis)**	**Results**	**T-car**
1 March	South African Grand Prix	Kyalami	11 Clay Regazzoni (312T/021) 12 Niki Lauda (312T/018)	Qualified 9th, Classified 16th Qualified 4th, Finished 5th	–
27 April	Spanish Grand Prix	Montjuich Park	11 Clay Regazzoni (312T/021) 12 Niki Lauda (312T/022)	Qualified 2nd, Finished NC Qualified 1st, DNF (accident)	312T/018
11 May	Monaco Grand Prix	Monaco	11 Clay Regazzoni (312T/018) 12 Niki Lauda (312T/023)	Qualified 6th, DNF (accident) Qualified 1st, Finished 1st	312T/021
25 May	Belgian Grand Prix	Zolder	11 Clay Regazzoni (312T/022) 12 Niki Lauda (312T/023)	Qualified 4th, Finished 5th Qualified 1st, Finished 1st	312T/018
8 June	Swedish Grand Prix	Anderstorpring	11 Clay Regazzoni (312T/021) 12 Niki Lauda (312T/023)	Qualified 4th, Finished 2nd Qualified 5th, Finished 1st	312T/022
22 June	Dutch Grand Prix	Zandvoort	11 Clay Regazzoni (312T/021) 12 Niki Lauda (312T/022)	Qualified 2nd, Finished 3rd Qualified 1st, Finished 2nd	312T/018
6 July	French Grand Prix	Dijon-Prenois	11 Clay Regazzoni (312T/024) 12 Niki Lauda (312T/022)	Qualified 9th, DNF (engine) Qualified 1st, Finished 1st	312T/018
19 July	British Grand Prix	Silverstone	11 Clay Regazzoni (312T/024) 12 Niki Lauda (312T/023)	Qualified 4th, Finished 13th Qualified 3rd, Finished 8th	312T/021
3 August	German Grand Prix	Nürburgring	11 Clay Regazzoni (312T/021) 12 Niki Lauda (312T/022)	Qualified 5th, DNF (engine) Qualified 1st, Finished 3rd	312T/018
17 August	Austrian Grand Prix	Österreichring	11 Clay Regazzoni (312T/024) 12 Niki Lauda (312T/022)	Qualified 5th, Finished 7th Qualified 1st, Finished 6th	312T/023
7 September	Italian Grand Prix	Monza	11 Clay Regazzoni (312T/024) 12 Niki Lauda (312T/023)	Qualified 2nd, Finished 1st Qualified 1st, Finished 3rd	312T/021
5 October	US Grand Prix	Watkins Glen	11 Clay Regazzoni (312T/024) 12 Niki Lauda (312T/023)	Qualified 11th, Withdrawn Qualified 1st, Finished 1st	312T/022

1976					
Date	**Race**	**Circuit**	**No. Driver (Chassis)**	**Results**	**T-car**
25 January	Brazilian Grand Prix	Interlagos	1 Niki Lauda (312T/023) 2 Clay Regazzoni (312T/024)	Qualified 2nd, Finished 1st Qualified 4th, Finished 7th	312T/022
6 March	South African Grand Prix	Kyalami	1 Niki Lauda (312T/023) 2 Clay Regazzoni (312T/022)	Qualified 2nd, Finished 1st Qualified 9th, DNF (engine)	312T/024
28 March	US Grand Prix West	Long Beach	1 Niki Lauda (312T/023) 2 Clay Regazzoni (312T/024)	Qualified 4th, Finished 2nd Qualified 1st, Finished 1st	312T/022
2 May	Spanish Grand Prix	Jarama	1 Niki Lauda (312T2/026) 2 Clay Regazzoni (312T2/025)	Qualified 2nd, Finished 2nd Qualified 5th, Finished 11th	312T/023
16 May	Belgian Grand Prix	Zolder	1 Niki Lauda (312T2/026) 2 Clay Regazzoni (312T2/025)	Qualified 1st, Finished 1st Qualified 2nd, Finished 2nd	312T/023
30 May	Monaco Grand Prix	Monaco	1 Niki Lauda (312T2/026) 2 Clay Regazzoni (312T2/027)	Qualified 1st, Finished 1st Qualified 2nd, Classified 14th	312T/025
13 June	Swedish Grand Prix	Anderstorpring	1 Niki Lauda (312T2/026) 2 Clay Regazzoni (312T2/027)	Qualified 5th, Finished 3rd Qualified 11th, Finished 6th	312T/025
4 July	French Grand Prix	Dijon-Prenois	1 Niki Lauda (312T2/026) 2 Clay Regazzoni (312T2/027)	Qualified 2nd, DNF (engine) Qualified 4th, DNF (spin)	312T/025

1976 (continued)					
Date	**Race**	**Circuit**	**No. Driver (Chassis)**	**Results**	**T-car**
18 July	British Grand Prix	Brands Hatch	1 Niki Lauda (312T2/028) 2 Clay Regazzoni (312T2/027)	Qualified 1st, Finished 2nd Qualified 4th, Disqualified	312T2/026
1 August	German Grand Prix	Nürburgring	1 Niki Lauda (312T2/028) 2 Clay Regazzoni (312T/025)	Qualified 2nd, DNF (accident) Qualified 5th, Finished 9th	312T2/026
29 August	Dutch Grand Prix	Zandvoort	2 Clay Regazzoni (312T2/027)	Qualified 5th, Finished 2nd	312T2/026
12 September	Italian Grand Prix	Monza	1 Niki Lauda (312T2/026) 2 Clay Regazzoni (312T2/027) 35 Carlos Reutemann (312T2/025)	Qualified 5th, Finished 4th Qualified 9th, Finished 2nd Qualified 7th, Finished 9th	312T2/023
3 October	Canadian Grand Prix	Mosport	1 Niki Lauda (312T2/026) 2 Clay Regazzoni (312T2/027)	Qualified 6th, Finished 8th Qualified 12th, Finished 6th	312T2/029
10 October	US Grand Prix	Watkins Glen	1 Niki Lauda (312T2/026) 2 Clay Regazzoni (312T2/027)	Qualified 5th, Finished 3rd Qualified 14th, Finished 7th	312T2/029
24 October	Japanese Grand Prix	Fuji	1 Niki Lauda (312T2/026) 2 Clay Regazzoni (312T2/027)	Qualified 3rd, DNF (withdrawn) Qualified 7th, Finished 5th	312T2/029

1977					
Date	**Race**	**Circuit**	**No. Driver (Chassis)**	**Results**	**T-car**
9 January	Argentine Grand Prix	Buenos Aires	11 Niki Lauda (312T2/026) 12 Carlos Reutemann (312T2/029)	Qualified 4th, DNF (engine) Qualified 7th, Finished 3rd	312T2/027
23 January	Brazilian Grand Prix	Interlagos	11 Niki Lauda (312T2/026) 12 Carlos Reutemann (312T2/029)	Qualified 13th, Finished 3rd Qualified 2nd, Finished 1st	312T2/027
5 March	South African Grand Prix	Kyalami	11 Niki Lauda (312T2/030) 12 Carlos Reutemann (312T2/027)	Qualified 3rd, Finished 1st Qualified 8th, Finished 8th	312T2/029
3 April	US Grand Prix West	Long Beach	11 Niki Lauda (312T2/030) 12 Carlos Reutemann (312T2/029)	Qualified 1st, Finished 2nd Qualified 4th, DNF (accident)	312T2/027
8 May	Spanish Grand Prix	Jarama	11 Niki Lauda (312T2/030) 12 Carlos Reutemann (312T2/029)	Qualified 3rd, DNS Qualified 4th, Finished 2nd	312T2/027
22 May	Monaco Grand Prix	Monaco	11 Niki Lauda (312T2/030) 12 Carlos Reutemann (312T2/029)	Qualified 6th, Finished 2nd Qualified 3rd, Finished 3rd	312T2/027
5 June	Belgian Grand Prix	Zolder	11 Niki Lauda (312T2/030) 12 Carlos Reutemann (312T2/029)	Qualified 11th, Finished 2nd Qualified 7th, DNF (accident)	312T2/027
19 June	Swedish Grand Prix	Anderstorpring	11 Niki Lauda (312T2/030) 12 Carlos Reutemann (312T2/029)	Qualified 15th, DNF (handling) Qualified 12th, Finished 3rd	312T2/027
3 July	French Grand Prix	Dijon-Prenois	11 Niki Lauda (312T2/031) 12 Carlos Reutemann (312T2/029)	Qualified 9th, Finished 5th Qualified 6th, Finished 6th	312T2/030
16 July	British Grand Prix	Silverstone	11 Niki Lauda (312T2/031) 12 Carlos Reutemann (312T2/029)	Qualified 3rd, Finished 2nd Qualified 14th, Finished 15th	312T2/027
31 July	German Grand Prix	Hockenheimring	11 Niki Lauda (312T2/031) 12 Carlos Reutemann (312T2/029)	Qualified 3rd, Finished 1st Qualified 8th, Finished 4th	312T2/027
14 August	Austrian Grand Prix	Österreichring	11 Niki Lauda (312T2/031) 12 Carlos Reutemann (312T2/029)	Qualified 1st, Finished 2nd Qualified 5th, Finished 4th	312T2/030
28 August	Dutch Grand Prix	Zandvoort	11 Niki Lauda (312T2/031) 12 Carlos Reutemann (312T2/029)	Qualified 4th, Finished 1st Qualified 6th, Finished 6th	312T2/030
11 September	Italian Grand Prix	Monza	11 Niki Lauda (312T2/031) 12 Carlos Reutemann (312T2/029)	Qualified 5th, Finished 2nd Qualified 2nd, DNF (accident)	312T2/030
2 October	US Grand Prix	Watkins Glen	11 Niki Lauda (312T2/031) 12 Carlos Reutemann (312T2/030)	Qualified 7th, Finished 4th Qualified 6th, Finished 6th	312T2/029
9 October	Canadian Grand Prix	Mosport	11 Niki Lauda 12 Carlos Reutemann (312T2/029) 21 Gilles Villeneuve (312T2/030)	Withdrawn Qualified 12th, DNF (fuel) Qualified 17th, Classified 12th	312T2/031
23 October	Japanese Grand Prix	Fuji	11 Gilles Villeneuve (312T2/030) 12 Carlos Reutemann (312T2/029)	Qualified 20th, DNF (accident) Qualified 7th, Finished 2nd	312T2/031

1978					
Date	**Race**	**Circuit**	**No. Driver (Chassis)**	**Results**	**T-car**
15 January	Argentine Grand Prix	Buenos Aires	11 Carlos Reutemann (312T2/031) 12 Gilles Villeneuve (312T2/027)	Qualified 2nd, Finished 7th Qualified 7th, Finished 8th	312T2/029
29 January	Brazilian Grand Prix	Interlagos	11 Carlos Reutemann (312T2/031) 12 Gilles Villeneuve (312T2/027)	Qualified 4th, Finished 1st Qualified 6th, DNF (accident)	312T2/029
4 March	South African Grand Prix	Kyalami	11 Carlos Reutemann (312T3/033) 12 Gilles Villeneuve (312T3/032)	Qualified 9th, DNF (accident) Qualified 8th, DNF (engine)	312T2/031
2 April	US Grand Prix West	Long Beach	11 Carlos Reutemann (312T3/032) 12 Gilles Villeneuve (312T3/034)	Qualified 1st, Finished 1st Qualified 2nd, DNF (accident)	312T3/033
7 May	Monaco Grand Prix	Monaco	11 Carlos Reutemann (312T3/032) 12 Gilles Villeneuve (312T3/034)	Qualified 1st, Finished 8th Qualified 8th, DNF (accident)	312T3/035
21 May	Belgian Grand Prix	Zolder	11 Carlos Reutemann (312T3/033) 12 Gilles Villeneuve (312T3/034)	Qualified 2nd, Finished 3rd Qualified 4th, Finished 4th	312T3/035
4 June	Spanish Grand Prix	Jarama	11 Carlos Reutemann (312T3/033) 12 Gilles Villeneuve (312T3/034)	Qualified 3rd, DNF (accident) Qualified 5th, Finished 10th	312T3/035
17 June	Swedish Grand Prix	Anderstorpring	11 Carlos Reutemann (312T3/036) 12 Gilles Villeneuve (312T3/034)	Qualified 8th, Finished 10th Qualified 7th, Finished 9th	312T3/035
2 July	French Grand Prix	Dijon-Prenois	11 Carlos Reutemann (312T3/036) 12 Gilles Villeneuve (312T3/035)	Qualified 8th, Finished 18th Qualified 9th, Finished 12th	312T3/034
16 July	British Grand Prix	Brands Hatch	11 Carlos Reutemann (312T3/033) 12 Gilles Villeneuve (312T3/034)	Qualified 8th, Finished 1st Qualified 13th, DNF (driveshaft)	312T3/036
30 July	German Grand Prix	Hockenheimring	11 Carlos Reutemann (312T3/033) 12 Gilles Villeneuve (312T3/035)	Qualified 12th, DNF (mechanical) Qualified 15th, Finished 8th	312T3/032
13 August	Austrian Grand Prix	Österreichring	11 Carlos Reutemann (312T3/036) 12 Gilles Villeneuve (312T3/034)	Qualified 4th, Disqualified Qualified 11th, Finished 3rd	312T3/035
27 August	Dutch Grand Prix	Zandvoort	11 Carlos Reutemann (312T3/036) 12 Gilles Villeneuve (312T3/034)	Qualified 4th, Finished 7th Qualified 5th, Finished 6th	312T3/035
10 September	Italian Grand Prix	Monza	11 Carlos Reutemann (312T3/036) 12 Gilles Villeneuve (312T3/034)	Qualified 11th, Finished 3rd Qualified 2nd, Finished 7th	312T3/035
1 October	US Grand Prix	Watkins Glen	11 Carlos Reutemann (312T3/035) 12 Gilles Villeneuve (312T3/034)	Qualified 2nd, Finished 1st Qualified 4th, DNF (engine)	312T3/036
8 October	Canadian Grand Prix	Montréal	11 Carlos Reutemann (312T3/035) 12 Gilles Villeneuve (312T3/034)	Qualified 11th, Finished 3rd Qualified 3rd, Finished 1st	312T3/036

1979					
Date	**Race**	**Circuit**	**No. Driver (Chassis)**	**Results**	**T-car**
21 January	Argentine Grand Prix	Buenos Aires	11 Jody Scheckter (312T3/035) 12 Gilles Villeneuve (312T3/036)	Qualified 5th, DNF (accident) Qualified 10th, Classified 12th	312T3/033
4 February	Brazilian Grand Prix	Interlagos	11 Jody Scheckter (312T3/035) 12 Gilles Villeneuve (312T3/034)	Qualified 6th, Finished 6th Qualified 5th, Finished 5th	312T3/033 312T3/036
3 March	South African Grand Prix	Kyalami	11 Jody Scheckter (312T4/038) 12 Gilles Villeneuve (312T4/037)	Qualified 2nd, Finished 2nd Qualified 3rd, Finished 1st	312T3/033
8 April	US Grand Prix West	Long Beach	11 Jody Scheckter (312T4/038) 12 Gilles Villeneuve (312T4/037)	Qualified 3rd, Finished 2nd Qualified 1st, Finished 1st	312T4/039
29 April	Spanish Grand Prix	Jarama	11 Jody Scheckter (312T4/039) 12 Gilles Villeneuve (312T4/037)	Qualified 5th, Finished 4th Qualified 3rd, Finished 7th	312T4/038
13 May	Belgian Grand Prix	Zolder	11 Jody Scheckter (312T4/040) 12 Gilles Villeneuve (312T4/039)	Qualified 7th, Finished 1st Qualified 6th, Classified 7th	312T4/038
27 May	Monaco Grand Prix	Monaco	11 Jody Scheckter (312T4/040) 12 Gilles Villeneuve (312T4/039)	Qualified 1st, Finished 1st Qualified 2nd, DNF (transmission)	312T4/038
1 July	French Grand Prix	Dijon-Prenois	11 Jody Scheckter (312T4/040) 12 Gilles Villeneuve (312T4/041)	Qualified 5th, Finished 7th Qualified 3rd, Finished 2nd	312T4/037
14 July	British Grand Prix	Silverstone	11 Jody Scheckter (312T4/039) 12 Gilles Villeneuve (312T4/038)	Qualified 11th, Finished 5th Qualified 13th, Classified 14th	312T4/037

1979 (continued)					
Date	**Race**	**Circuit**	**No. Driver (Chassis)**	**Results**	**T-car**
29 July	German Grand Prix	Hockenheimring	11 Jody Scheckter (312T4/040) 12 Gilles Villeneuve (312T4/041)	Qualified 5th, Finished 4th Qualified 9th, Finished 8th	312T4/039
12 August	Austrian Grand Prix	Österreichring	11 Jody Scheckter (312T4/040) 12 Gilles Villeneuve (312T4/041)	Qualified 9th, Finished 4th Qualified 5th, Finished 2nd	312T4/038
26 August	Dutch Grand Prix	Zandvoort	11 Jody Scheckter (312T4/040) 12 Gilles Villeneuve (312T4/041)	Qualified 5th, Finished 2nd Qualified 6th, DNF (suspension)	312T4/039
9 September	Italian Grand Prix	Monza	11 Jody Scheckter (312T4/040) 12 Gilles Villeneuve (312T4/038)	Qualified 3rd, Finished 1st Qualified 5th, Finished 2nd	312T4/037
30 September	Canadian Grand Prix	Montréal	11 Jody Scheckter (312T4/040) 12 Gilles Villeneuve (312T4/041)	Qualified 9th, Finished 4th Qualified 2nd, Finished 2nd	312T4/038
7 October	US Grand Prix	Watkins Glen	11 Jody Scheckter (312T4/040) 12 Gilles Villeneuve (312T4/041)	Qualified 16th, DNF (puncture) Qualified 3rd, Finished 1st	312T4/038

1980					
Date	**Race**	**Circuit**	**No. Driver (Chassis)**	**Results**	**T-car**
13 January	Argentine Grand Prix	Buenos Aires	1 Jody Scheckter (312T5/042) 2 Gilles Villeneuve (312T5/043)	Qualified 11th, DNF (engine) Qualified 8th, DNF (accident)	312T5/044
27 January	Brazilian Grand Prix	Interlagos	1 Jody Scheckter (312T5/042) 2 Gilles Villeneuve (312T5/045)	Qualified 8th, DNF (engine) Qualified 3rd, Classified 16th	312T5/044
1 March	South African Grand Prix	Kyalami	1 Jody Scheckter (312T5/046) 2 Gilles Villeneuve (312T5/042)	Qualified 9th, DNF (engine) Qualified 10th, DNF (transmission)	312T5/045
30 March	US Grand Prix West	Long Beach	1 Jody Scheckter (312T5/046) 2 Gilles Villeneuve (312T5/045)	Qualified 16th, Finished 5th Qualified 10th, DNF (driveshaft)	312T5/042
4 May	Belgian Grand Prix	Zolder	1 Jody Scheckter (312T5/046) 2 Gilles Villeneuve (312T5/045)	Qualified 14th, Finished 8th Qualified 12th, Finished 6th	312T5/044
18 May	Monaco Grand Prix	Monaco	1 Jody Scheckter (312T5/046) 2 Gilles Villeneuve (312T5/045)	Qualified 17th, DNF (handling) Qualified 6th, Finished 5th	312T5/044
1 June	Spanish Grand Prix	Jarama	1 Jody Scheckter (312T5/046) 2 Gilles Villeneuve (312T5/044)	Withdrawn Withdrawn	312T5/045
29 June	French Grand Prix	Paul Ricard	1 Jody Scheckter (312T5/046) 2 Gilles Villeneuve (312T5/045)	Qualified 19th, Finished 12th Qualified 17th, Finished 8th	312T5/044
13 July	British Grand Prix	Brands Hatch	1 Jody Scheckter (312T5/046) 2 Gilles Villeneuve (312T5/045)	Qualified 23rd, Finished 10th Qualified 19th, DNF (engine)	312T5/044
10 August	German Grand Prix	Hockenheimring	1 Jody Scheckter (312T5/046) 2 Gilles Villeneuve (312T5/048)	Qualified 21st, Finished 13th Qualified 16th, Finished 6th	312T5/045
17 August	Austrian Grand Prix	Österreichring	1 Jody Scheckter (312T5/044) 2 Gilles Villeneuve (312T5/043)	Qualified 22nd, Finished 13th Qualified 15th, Finished 8th	312T5/045
31 August	Dutch Grand Prix	Zandvoort	1 Jody Scheckter (312T5/046) 2 Gilles Villeneuve (312T5/048)	Qualified 12th, Finished 9th Qualified 7th, Finished 7th	312T5/045
14 September	Italian Grand Prix	Imola	1 Jody Scheckter (312T5/043) 2 Gilles Villeneuve (312T5/048)	Qualified 16th, Finished 8th Qualified 8th, DNF (accident)	312T5/045 312T5/046
28 September	Canadian Grand Prix	Montréal	1 Jody Scheckter (312T5/043) 2 Gilles Villeneuve (312T5/045*)	DNQ Qualified 22nd, Finished 5th	312T5/044*
5 October	US Grand Prix	Watkins Glen	1 Jody Scheckter (312T5/044) 2 Gilles Villeneuve (312T5/043)	Qualified 23rd, Finished 11th Qualified 18th, DNF (accident)	312T5/045

*Switched to 044 for the restart after 045 was damaged in first lap accident.

Appendix 3

Ferrari 312T series non-championship race history

Date	Race	Circuit	No. Driver (Chassis)	Results	Team
1975					
13 April	BRDC International Trophy	Silverstone	12 Niki Lauda (312T/022)	Qualified 2nd, Finished 1st	Scuderia Ferrari
24 August	Swiss Grand Prix	Dijon-Prenois	12 Clay Regazzoni (312T/021)	Qualified 3rd, Finished 1st	Scuderia Ferrari
1976					
14 March	Race of Champions	Brands Hatch	1 Niki Lauda (312T2/025) 36 Giancarlo Martini (312T/021)	Qualified 2nd, DNF (brakes) Qualified 15th, DNS (crash on warm-up lap)	Scuderia Ferrari Scuderia Everest
11 April	BRDC International Trophy	Silverstone	39 Giancarlo Martini (312T/021)	Qualified 10th, Finished 10th	Scuderia Everest
1979					
15 April	Race of Champions	Brands Hatch	12 Gilles Villeneuve (312T3/033)	Qualified 3rd, Finished 1st	Scuderia Ferrari
16 September	Gran Premio Dino Ferrari	Imola	11 Jody Scheckter (312T4/037) 12 Gilles Villeneuve (312T4/038)	Qualified 2nd, Finished 3rd Qualified 1st, Finished 7th	Scuderia Ferrari Scuderia Ferrari

Appendix 4

Ferrari 312T series race wins by chassis

312T/023	6 wins (1975 Monaco GP, 1975 Belgian GP, 1975 Swedish GP, 1975 US GP, 1976 Brazilian GP, 1976 South African GP)
312T2/031	3 wins (1977 Dutch GP, 1977 US GP, 1978 Brazilian GP)
312T4/040	3 wins (1979 Belgian GP, 1979 Monaco GP, 1979 Italian GP)
312T/022	2 wins (1975 Dutch GP, 1975 French GP)
312T/024	2 wins (1975 Italian GP, 1976 US GP West)
312T2/026	2 wins (1976 Belgian GP, 1976 Monaco GP)
312T4/037	2 wins (1979 South African GP, 1979 US GP West)
312T3/032	1 win (1978 US GP West)
312T3/033	1 win (1978 British GP)
312T3/034	1 win (Canadian GP)
312T3/035	1 win (1978 US GP East)
312T4/041	1 win (1979 US GP East)

Appendix 5

Drivers' Championship results

1975	Niki Lauda	1st	64.5 points
	Clay Regazzoni	5th	25 points
1976	Niki Lauda	2nd	68 points
	Clay Regazzoni	5th	31 points
1977	Niki Lauda	1st	72 points
	Carlos Reutemann	4th	42 points
	Gilles Villeneuve	–	0 points
1978	Carlos Reutemann	3rd	48 points
	Gilles Villeneuve	9th	17 points
1979	Jody Scheckter	1st	51 points
	Gilles Villeneuve	2nd	47 points
1980	Jody Scheckter	19th	2 points
	Gilles Villeneuve	14th	6 points

Appendix 6

Constructors' Championship results

1975	1st	72.5 points
1976	1st	83 points
1977	1st	95 points
1978	2nd	58 points
1979	1st	113 points
1980	10th	8 points

Appendix 7

Useful contacts

Adams McCall Engineering
The Workshop
Home Farm Laverstoke Park
Nr Whitchurch
Hampshire RG28 7NT
Tel +44 (0)1256 771666
Preparation

Avon Tyres Motorsport
Bath Road
Melksham
Wiltshire, SN12 8AA
Tel +44 (0)1225 703101
Tyres

Bonhams
101 New Bond Street
London W1S 1SR
Tel +44 (0)207 468 8200
Auctioneers

Coys
Manor Court
Lower Mortlake Road
Richmond TW9 2LL
Tel +44 (0) 208 614 7888
Auctioneers

Duncan Hamilton & Co
PO Box 222
Hook
Nr Basingstoke
Hampshire RG27 9YZ
Tel +44 (0) 1256 765000
Sales

Ellis Clowes
27 Horse Fair
Banbury
Oxfordshire OX16 0AE
Tel +44 (0) 1295 221190
Insurance

Ferrari Classiche
Maranello Sales Ltd
Tower Garage
A30 By-Pass
Egham
Surrey TW20 0AX
Tel +44 (0) 1784 558423
Certification and authentication

FIA
Historic Department
2 Chemin de Blandonnet
Case Postale 296
1215 Geneva 15 Airport
Switzerland
Technical regulation and administration

Goodwood
Will Kinsman
The Goodwood Estate
Chichester
West Sussex
PO18 0PX
Tel +44 (0) 1243 755000
Competitors' enquiries

Goose Live Events
Sweetapple House
Catteshall Road
Godalming
Surrey GU7 3DJ
Tel +44 (0) 1483 524400
Event organiser

Hagerty International
The Arch Barn
Oury Hill Farm
Towcester
Northamptonshire
NN12 7TB
Tel +44 (0)844 8241130
Insurance

Hall & Hall
Graham Hill Way
Cherry Holt Road
Bourne
Lincolnshire
PE10 9PJ
Tel +44 (0) 1778 392561
Preparation

Historic Grand Prix
4 Finch Road
North Salem
NY10560
USA
Race organisation

Masters Historic Racing
The Bunker
Lower End Road
Wavendon
Milton Keynes
MK17 8DA
Tel +44 (0)1908 587545
Championship management

Phil Reilly & Company
5842 Paradise Drive
Corte Madera
CA94925
USA
Tel +1 (415) 924 9022
Preparation

RM/Sotheby's
One Classic Car Drive
Blenheim
Ontario N0P 1A0
Canada
Tel +1 519 352 4575
Auctioneers

Stuart McCrudden Associates
West Hall
Lea Lane
Great Baxted
Witham
Essex CM8 3EP
Tel +44 (0)1621 892814
Race organisation

ABOVE There are many helping hands available to help you to enjoy your 312T series. *(Author)*

Index